WHEN THE STUDENT IS READY

THE AWAKENING OF SPIRITUAL CONSCIOUSNESS

VOLUME 1

By

MICHAEL E. CLARKE

Published by: Michael E. Clarke
Website: www.MichaelEClarke.com
Copyright©2016 Michael E. Clarke

Cover Artwork © Peter Rogers

REVIEWS FOR
"WHEN THE STUDENT IS READY"

"*When the Student is Ready* provides golden nuggets of spiritual truths for its readers. The author challenges you to live life consciously and responsibly as you create the life of your dreams. I have been on my spiritual path of awareness for over thirty years, and I repeatedly felt resonance with what I read. This book is an ideal distillation of spiritual wisdom and explains the author's journey of growth. Here you will find breadcrumbs to guide you on your unique trail to self-discovery and higher consciousness."

Gail Saunders
#1 International Bestselling author of Resilient Heart: Transcending the Death of Your Loved One. Gail is a resilient catalyst as a transition coach and author of transformation books. GailSaunders.com

"Michael is a progressive and highly elevated thinker and spiritualist. His work transcends the limits of religion and scientific understanding and takes the reader to an evolving journey of wisdom, insight, and light speed clairvoyance. His book will answer questions for you that you have not even formulated in your head. The universe led me to his work, and I am excited for all those who will be blessed to read him. Highly recommended."

Dr. Sana Rafig-Mitchell, Ed.D
Leadership consultant and professional Editor

"Reading this book touched places within myself that had not only been asleep, these were places within myself had never had a spiritually awakening at all. If you have ever felt "Flat Lined" in your day to day life, you may very well get a glimmer of the mystery beginning to unfold within this insightful book. Take your time with it and enjoy!"

Debbie Nix

Life Coach, CEO, <u>PassionDrivenLiving.Com</u>

"I feel overwhelmed with emotions as I read this beautifully written book. This book will take you on a journey through the most important topics of all: co-creation and self-realization. I can sense a soul connection as I read and listen within; my inner guidance joins in, and the voice of truth lights up and dissolves all illusions. I have no doubt that this book has been written and handled carefully under the crystal-clear light of the soul. This book is a true gift to anyone who considers himself/herself on the path of the beautiful truth of being."

Mohamed Omar

Founder of *Intentional Beings & The Seven Simple Steps |*
The Natural Path of Co-Creation & Self-Realization.

<u>intentionalbeings.com</u>

TABLE OF CONTENTS

DEDICATION

This book is dedicated to my great aunt, Jane Clarke, who was both my spiritual guide post and dear second mother to me, and to my mother and father who separately provided the spark that allowed my personality to emerge. To all of my family for always being there for me, and to my incredible friends for providing the stable environment that helped me grow and discover my true self.

Most of all, this book is dedicated to my daughters: Whitney and Stefanie. What started as hundreds of random pieces of paper, finally came into form. My original intent was to get my experiences and broadening perspective on paper so that my girls might benefit someday. The book ultimately took on a life of its own. Without my girls, this book would not have happened. I love you both so much.

I also dedicate this book to all of the seekers of truth, for without the quest for a better understanding of life, we slowly drift off course. This book is meant to be a guide towards a higher perspective and an understanding of why things are the way they are, and more importantly, understand how our beliefs form our reality. It is when the student is ready, that these messages become clear. Thank you so much for sharing in this journey.

PREFACE

In this book, I'll be talking about various elements of consciousness, creation, science, and even some social justifications that we have incorporated into our daily rituals. In general, we'll discuss the common elements of science, religion and the spiritual views that greatly impact how we experience our lives. This inquiry includes the creation of our existence, as well as the creation of our personal desires through our ever-evolving conscious awareness. Hopefully, through some of these conciderations, we'll cultivate a seed of curiosity that may someday awaken your dormant curiosity. What the seed grows into is always your choice.

"When the student is ready," is a metaphor for an internal acceptance. This acceptance means that we've taken responsibility for the cultivation of our personal quest for higher awareness.

This book is not an attempt to tell you what to think; there's enough of that going on around us every day. This is an attempt to get you *to think bigger*.

We've been conditioned to believe that happiness resides within our relationships, financial security, or even our faith. All of these things can, and often do change. However, awareness gained from an inward journey becomes a part of you forever. Inner awareness cannot be taken away; you cannot unsee the seen or un-experience the experience.

Part of your new awareness on this journey will be a shift in thinking. You will no longer expect the things that you do, will change who you are. You will come to realize that you must first change who you are, to change what you do. Your inner awareness will ultimately define what you create yourself to be.

Another significant shift in awareness will be to thoroughly understand that we really can't *change* anyone. We can only facilitate that person in their desire to change. Trying to "fix" someone will always be an exercise in futility. Even as people may ask for help, they're not likely to fully understand the depth of the solution, until they acquire the depth of understanding needed to connect the new information to their old belief. So, analogous to the old aphorism, until the student is ready, the teacher isn't of much use.

Unfortunately, most of us have become numb over time by a multitude of authoritative conditionings including our parents, teachers, governments, and even some religions. Because of this spectrum of authority figures, our lives have been predominately operated out of some level of subconscious fear. Authority figures know when they insist on conformity, they create control; consequently, we've been funneled into limited points of view that support this structure.

Morality, for example, is less taught as an unfolding of one's virtue, than it is taught as a commandment to conform. This is how fear is imposed. Interestingly though, the people within these systems generally don't *see* the fear in their choice, they just see the justification for moral regulation. These people see their "choice" as sound and rational, yet most likely, the subconscious reason for their choice is rooted in fear of retribution. As a whole, people see their *intent* as their choice... but they seldom see that *their choice* is a version of someone else's rule, adopted as their belief. Any fear-based decision will hold you back. One of the objectives of this book is to show you where your fears come from and how to overcome them.

Free thinkers have often been considered dangerous; history validates this. There have been many great teachers and philosophers throughout history that were killed attempting to elevate the consciousness of man.

Conform! Don't rock the boat or there's hell to pay! ... literally. This mashing down of curiosity has softened man's desire to seek the truth for fear of retribution on numerous levels. We feel guilty for questioning authority. We settle for jobs that we feel stuck in. We settle for dysfunctional relationships because they are better than being alone. We're driven to succeed, but we also want peace and a sense of well-being. We want security, but we also want to expand our consciousness, all of which humans have been doing throughout time.

All of this structure has created a tiny box for us to comfortably exist within. This is why few people venture very far from these imposed conventional boundaries. Fear of ridicule keeps them on the very straight and narrow path.

There *will*, however, come a day when the curious will venture out. The questions will outnumber the answers, and the truth will become the quest. Only when our hearts and our minds are primed with curiosity can we see the light. This is why I chose the title for this book, *"When the Student is Ready."* Through my quest to expand my personal awareness, I was able to see sides of things that most people haven't seen yet, sometimes because they don't want to, and sometimes because they just haven't looked.

I don't offer this as an absolute; I simply offer a perspective that if not considered, can't be experienced. This is why an accurate perception of something requires notable effort to conceive all sides. This applies to the physical and non-physical. Everyone and everything have many perspectives to consider before a clear picture of the whole can be seen, or better yet, understood.

The purpose of this book is to show you how your beliefs and perceptions shape your reality. The concepts within this book *will* shed new light to some of your long-held beliefs, and I will discuss how Science and Spirituality are beginning to uncover the same "Big Picture."

Our efforts towards emotional or spiritual healing must begin with an internal quest. Once you understand where real change comes from, you'll know where to focus your efforts.

This book was originally intended as a guide for my kids. I wanted to leave something behind that expressed and explained what I had experienced during my life. It was to be a sampling of personal revelations, concepts that might help explain life in a way that most people don't talk much about. I also knew that I had opened doors into my mind that most people wouldn't venture through. These were doors, not only into my soul, but doors into multiple dimensions and alternate realities. This book is my attempt to share these revelations in an effort to spark an inquisition towards your own quest for enlightenment.

The previous image referenced from
Weisstein, Eric W. "Young girl - old woman."
From MathWorld—A Wolfram Web Resource.
http://mathworld.com/younggirl-oldwomanIllusion.html

THE BIG PICTURE

Without looking back at the previous picture, what did you see? This image is a great depiction of how seldom we see all of what is right in front of us. This picture contains two images. One image is of an old lady, and the other image is of a beautiful maiden. You may be able to see both images, but many people can only see one or the other. Here's one reason why; our brains are conditioned to stop looking for new information once we think we think we've found an answer. In this example, your brain was unaware that there were multiple answers, and likely only saw one image, then stopped looking. Now, if you knew ahead of time that there were two images, your brain would automatically look for both images.

Here's why this is relevant. Throughout history and up until this very moment, we have been conditioned to look at life in one specific way or another. You've been told that reality is a constant and that this reality is yours. Consequently, you've never even started to search for many of the key elements of life that are critical to your spiritual and emotional evolution. These keys to our very existence are embedded within each and every experience and surround us at every turn, and yet we're oblivious to their mere existence. This is not your fault; you were never even told to look. For the most part, these "additional pieces of the big picture" have been obscured from your discovery or glossed over as a waste of time, or even blasphemy.

The objective here is only to point out that there will always be exponentially more to life than what may seem to be right in front of our face. Once we start to look past what we're "supposed" to see, we can then begin to look towards what we might see. This is where self-discovery begins.

INTRODUCTION

I am not a biblical scholar, nor do I claim to be a scholar of any religion. I am a man seeking the truth. My experiences have shown that the truth does not exist within any single belief; the truth lies within the desire to find it. This book represents a personal revelation of how a consciously lived life provides both the experiences and the means necessary to discover your higher purpose for this life.

This book is not about what you *should* do; it's about learning to re-create your life by expanding your conscious awareness. This book is also not about criticizing one's personal beliefs. We will each make moves in the direction that we feel drawn when ready. At some point though, we must begin to question our place in this universe or we will leave this life experience without any real progress towards enlightenment. If you're comfortable with your current view of the world, then this book probably isn't for you. However, if your curiosity is telling you to look a little deeper, then this book should help satisfy why you feel that way. You are an integral part of something much greater than your current understanding. My intention here is to clarify some universal spiritual principals that were realized through my personal quest for a broader perspective. The primary purpose of this book is to help you see through the limiting beliefs that have prevented you from experiencing your yet untapped higher self. You'll find that some of the things that didn't quite make sense before will finally come together. There is an underlying unification to everything.

One simple shift in consciousness will allow for a much clearer perspective. This transformational shift in perspective shows us that we are not separate from anything, ever, especially our source. It'll take a very diligent effort on your part to expand your current vision. The truth is not in a lesson or in any book; it comes from experiencing your life from a much broader perspective. It won't be a perspective based on any belief; it will be a perspective built out of your evolving higher awareness. The more questions you ask, the more answers you'll find. You'll see that finding is far different than reading, and you'll soon find that your new awareness will produce more evolved experiences. This is why the title of this book is so descriptive. As you become prepared for the truth, the truth will find you.

What I write about is not a religious belief. This book is simply a broader perspective of life, based on ancient teachings, science, philosophy and modern spirituality that transcends any singular religion or belief. The truth transcends any singular path. My intention is not to persuade anyone of anything, nor can I teach you anything. I can only share from within myself what you must discover within yourself.

What was revealed to me, as I stretched my narrow views, was that God is not a finite entity to be believed in, but rather that God is the *process* of creation through its inherent collective intelligence. The revelation of God as the process of *creation*, not the Creator, neatly pulled all the scattered puzzle pieces of Truth together.

Jesus states, "One must seek first the Kingdom and all will be added unto you." When we seek the truth through greater awareness, we discover that the *truth* is everywhere and within everything. The truth exists within our desire to learn.

The Buddha teaches that there is no knowledge without sacrifice. The truth is revealed on one's curious path, and there is no destination. The Tao Te Ching states that to only seek physical form is not to know the truth. The truth is neither the named nor the nameless, yet it is both. It is the essence *within* and *of* everything. The Kingdom of Heaven is not a place, it's a state of being, and the truth is a gift that's opened with each curious step we take.

Religions are not bad; they are just independent attempts at a finite definable truth, and they have led us to where we are now.

My spiritual path has taken many forms for over twenty-five years. More importantly, I put myself through numerous intense spiritual training processes that ultimately challenged my fundamental understanding. As a student of truth, I was seeking the essence of each newly studied philosophy. My objective was to divine the essence and the intention behind the words and experiences that I encountered.

Each newly acquired perspective allowed me to lift a piece

of the veil and experience a broader view of an ever-expanding reality. Each new philosophy contributed another piece of the big picture; many of the concepts were like puzzle pieces made of puzzle pieces. Each of the pieces uniquely demonstrated an infinite path to the past and at the same time, continually showed new ways to experience life.

The underlying realities of our traditional faiths have been torn apart. One has but to *pull together* the multitude of scattered pieces to find the truth again.

When one stops to disseminate how religions evolved from original truth, it's easy then to reconcile the truth within each religion. The Truth needs no agenda, and the Truth makes no rules. The natural laws of life work without exception.

The Tao Te Ching states, "The Tao that can be spoken is not the true Tao." To define God is not to know God. The unknown will always be greater than the known. We must accept the unknown as our quest and relish in its discovery. Trying to define what's around the unseen corner is ultimately what limits the experience. We must release our desire to define what we think we know and allow the mysteries of life to unfold.

Not surprisingly, science has finally proved the interconnected nature of energy and life, but even with all their advanced technology, they still don't grasp the nature of consciousness. Physicists don't seem to recognize consciousness with any quantitative value at all. So far, I believe that consciousness is considered nonscientific. Scientists will mention the "word" consciousness, but not as a living component of life or a quantifiable concept. Instead, physicists talk about gravity as being the universal operating system. In their paradigm, gravity is the force that holds everything together. In reality, consciousness is the universal operating system that gravity and everything else exists within. Absolutely everything exists inside of something else and gravity is the effect, not the cause.

In science, there was nothing before the Big Bang. In religion, there was nothing before the Word. The only thing that could exist before Matter, is the desire to exist.

Before the Word, there is thought, and before thought, their consciousness. At the moment of our universal existence, a collective consciousness is born. Through our collective desire to exist, we evolve individually. This innate desire to exist is the process of creation itself.

This is certainly a quantum shift in understanding from where most people stand now. This shift was arduous for me as well. My quest had challenged most of the allegories that had previously offered me comfort.

It was my resolve to stay open to what was finally beginning to make sense that kept me moving forward. Another thing that added viability to my quest was how science was validating our understanding of energy and its inherent intelligence. With *Religious* common threads now pulled tight, I grew to see every living and nonliving thing as interconnected and all from the same God source. We are all individual expressions of the process of creation. We are all interconnected!

This essence, which we call soul, spirit, mind, and humanity, are all evolving from a direct reflection of benevolent love expressing itself as life. A flower doesn't grow by commandment; it simply emerges to fulfill its evolving nature. It's through this universal cooperative effort that all of life emerges and evolves. Our energy and our essence are connected to our bodies, yet they are not bound to our bodies.

We exist throughout multiple dimensions simultaneously. The "Heaven" that we all share is not a place of attainment; it is the source of our evolving spirit, and the dimension to which we all return. Jesus affirms this when he states, "The Kingdom of God does not come with observation, nor will they see it here or there, but the kingdom of Heaven is within."

This is a much bigger picture of what God is or isn't, and it allows for infinite individual creation. When Jesus stated, "these things and more ye shall also do" he was describing our divine nature and our ability to create through *will*.

I eventually embodied the awareness that this deeper, multidimensional world of life, *all mattered*, and that our deeper purpose in life is to grasp the implications of our ever-evolving spirit. Every experience matters and each experience in life is a building block for the next experience. We can only grow experientially, and it's through our conscious act of creation that we fulfill our higher purpose. In doing so, we contribute collectively to the evolution of everything.

As you read forward, consider in how many ways you may have limited yourself. Your jobs, your relationships and more importantly, your personal development are all tied to your beliefs. As you begin to release these tethers of fear-based decisions you can begin to experience a realm of possibilities that were simply not visible before. Our universal source is always working within us. Not out of judgment or commandment, but out of the universal principles that bind us all together. The purpose in life is not learning how to get through it, but how to embrace it. We're not here to avoid conflict. We're here to discover our potential through each experience.

You will discover that we are infinitely interconnected throughout dimensions, and that we create ourselves through our evolving relationship with all of life. You will learn to see yourself through the eyes of creation, and you'll experience how your personal connection with universal spirit provides the guidance for your personal quest for higher consciousness.

There's a lot of books out there designed to help you make more money, find more happiness or have a better relationship, but the most important thing is to find happiness where you are. The purpose of this book is to help you see the beauty in where you are right now. Once you've discovered your true inner self, you can then create or follow any path you desire. These new paths won't be a search for happiness; these paths will reveal your joy and inner peace. This is when your eyes truly become open, and the purpose in this life experience becomes clear.

You'll see how each step in life matters. You'll see how each experience adds context and direction to your evolving life, and how everything affects everything.

Hopefully, this book will ignite a spark of curiosity that sets forth your path. We each have our own path, however, each path not taken will wait. When you, the Student, is ready, your path will beckon you, and your quest will begin.

Thank you so much for sharing this experience!

When the grace of our spirit is felt by another, we lift in their soul the feeling of hope, and when we share even a glimmer of hope, we raise the vibration of love in the world.

THE QUEST

I've learned not to take much of anything at its face value anymore. I try to consider the intent behind almost everything, and this is how my quest began. When I turned thirty years old, over twenty-five years ago, I had achieved most of the major goals that I had set out for myself. I owned a nice home, owned my own business, was married and had two beautiful children. Despite these obvious symbols of modern well-being and stability, I felt an absolute compulsion to *know* more.

I had always been devout in my Christian faith, and never had a reason or impulse to question anything about it. Nevertheless, the religion that I was raised in was *now* a topic up for debate. Not by someone else, this was happening in my head, and I didn't understand why. I felt a compulsive obligation to dig deeper. My family was a typical Christian family. Not overly zealous, just the basic stuff. Heaven, hell, Jesus, the Ten Commandments, all the usual do's and dont's. By eighth grade, I had joined the Fellowship of Christian Athletes and surrounded myself with an even more devout crowd. I had been "saved," "born again," spoke in tongues, all that fun stuff. I would even sit on the curb at night with one of my friends in high school and talk about the Bible. That's what Christians did, right? I was definitely on a path conditioned by my environment and upbringing. At the time there didn't seem much else to consider. I think that his is how most of us move from one phase of life to the other; for the most part, we move with the crowd.

Well, there was an incident that happened while I was in high school that I later recognized as a major life altering event. This pivotal moment turned out to be a major course correction. I believe that we are always guided in directions that help keep us on *our* chosen path; meaning that our free will is still in play, but we are being reminded that we had an objective to accomplish in this life experience and have been pointed back in that direction. There were many course correcting events throughout my life that all played a part in my spiritual awakening. I'll tell you this one because it played such an integral part in forming the next three decades of my life.

I was a Sophomore in high school and got a job at a produce market quite a few miles away from my house. I believe my mother helped me find the job. There was a lot to learn about the produce business, and it came with a lot of responsibility. I was a conscientious kid and always like to learn new things. Within a few months of working with the owner, I had learned enough to run the small market by myself. It was a very quiet little market, and I enjoyed visiting with the local customers that frequented the place. I also learned a lot more about Greens than you could imagine. I had more than a couple of "discussions" on the difference between turnip and collard greens with some of my regulars. It was a fun place to work for sure.

After a short while of working at the market by myself, the

owner's daughter who was my age started to come by to hang out. She started to come by more and more frequently, and we were definitely on a collision course towards a relationship. We were definitely "hitting it off." Well, one day a girlfriend of hers came to the market to visit. She was very friendly, and we all had a great time laughing and carrying on. Near the end of that afternoon, I had mentioned that my car was in the shop and that I would have to call home for a ride after we closed. Her friend gladly offered me a ride home because she lived in the same area that I did, and of course, I accepted the ride home. I couldn't have known it at the time, but this was going to be a major adjustment in my life's direction.

I know that each moment in life gives us the opportunity to choose our path, but this particular path seemed to jump out in front of me. This was certainly my choice to make, but the choice seemed to be making itself.

After we had got to my house, we sat in the driveway and talked for what may have been an hour or more. She leaned over to kiss me and we were instantly connected. We wound up dating through the rest of our high school years and had even begun small talk about our long-term plans.

(This next part of the story would establish the framework for the next phase.)

Being a conscientious young man, but one without any money, I'd had the forethought to acknowledge that if I were ever to get married, I would need a ring. Even though this was certainly not imminent, I started looking around. I found a jewelry store close by that had a layaway plan and started making payments on a .63ct diamond. It was an attractive round cut diamond of a quality that I could afford. I stopped by every few weeks for quite a few months to make the payments in person. I met with the owner on most of the visits and had a very friendly relationship with him. I think he enjoyed helping out with this bright idea of mine.

The summer after I had graduated from high school I was at a local mall when I ran into the jewelry store owner that I had bought my diamond from. We stopped to visit for a while, and he asked me what I was doing for the summer. Looking for work, I smiled. He told me that he was opening a jewelry manufacturing operation and would I be interested in learning how to make jewelry. Heck yeah! was my answer, and I started to work that next week.

This subtle shift in who I might meet and would date in high school would turn out to have a monumental effect on the direction of my life. Had I not accepted the ride home that day, I would have likely taken an entirely different path with its own set of possible directions. Dating the business owner's daughter would have come with an entirely different set of options. Anyway, I didn't know it at the time, but I had just started a career in the jewelry industry that would last for nearly 30 years. By the way, the diamond that I had purchased earlier was never put to use. My high school girlfriend and I parted ways soon after high school. I eventually sold the diamond to pay for other life necessities. My high school relationship had served its purpose well, and it was now time to start the next phase of my life. I think everything worked out just fine.

After only a year in the jewelry business, I had learned how to do most of the individual components of jewelry manufacturing. At the age of 19 years old I was managing the manufacturing part of this business; there were about 18 employees at the time. It was at this point that I saw the jewelry business as a potential career path. With the help of my great Aunt, I was able to attend the Gemological Institute of America in Santa Monica California to get my Graduate Gemologist certification. At the age of twenty-six, I was able to start my own company and would go on to invent and patent the first ever home use jewelry steam cleaner. I was fortunate enough to launch my steamer on all of the major television home shopping channels. My steamer was distributed throughout the jewelry industry as well. This path enabled me to help a few other companies with the manufacturing and distribution of their own products.

Remember now, that this whole path was a result of accepting a ride from a friend of a friend.

At this point in my life, I had accomplished most of the things that I had set out to do. As an adult, I was used to putting in hard work and having something to show for it. I owned my own home, and I owned my own business. I even got my pilots license and bought a plane with a business partner. I liked the idea of creating things, and I liked helping people. I seemed to be well suited for what I was doing. However, after my children were grown and off on their own, I had begun to sense something within myself that I couldn't quite explain. It felt like I was being pulled away. Not drawn to something, but an actual feeling of being pulled away. The best way to describe this feeling was that it felt like a big hot air balloon fully inflated yet tethered to the ground. It was pulling hard, and there didn't seem to be any logical reason for it.

Searching for answers, I was forced back in my mind to the spiritual lessons that had been passed on to me from my great Aunt, Jane Clarke. She certainly wouldn't have called herself a Guru, but ultimately, this was to be one of her major roles in my life.

I'll take you through what her many years of mentoring meant for me while I was growing up. My Aunt Jane was, by far, the most influential and spiritual person that I knew at this point in my life. She was my spiritual guidepost. She was a strong woman with a good mind for business as well as being the, "go to" person if you needed help. She had helped me in so many ways and had helped many others in our family as well. She helped refugees from other countries along with almost anyone else that needed her. She was a rock of inspiration for many, and a source of hope for a lot more.

In elementary school, I was often around her house when she held her monthly meditation classes and discussion groups. I didn't understand much of what they were talking about at the time, but in retrospect, I knew that being exposed to her philosophy and passion for life was no accident on any level.

She provided a home for six very large spiritual paintings that ranged from seven to nine feet tall. There was not doubt that they made a statement, both by their size, and their content. This spiritual series that metaphorically depicted the evolution of spiritual consciousness was appropriately titled, "The Quest," by acclaimed English Artist, Peter Rogers. Peter's personal spiritual revelation is what compelled him to paint this inspiring series that he still paints today. Peter and my Aunt Jane arranged to have the paintings reside at her house if she would build the space for them to be displayed and appreciated. She accepted the challenge.

My Aunt Jane was already a spiritual teacher and taught in churches and many other venues. She was now taking the next step in her personal spiritual journey. She began a construction project that would ultimately be known as, "The Sun Room." This is where Peter Rogers' series of paintings, "The Quest," would reside for nearly twenty years. These paintings provided the backdrop of inspiration for many people in so many ways.

Shortly after my 30th birthday, my questions multiplied dramatically. Although I had been taught not to question my religion, I cautiously, but diligently, began to tip-toe around a new way of thinking about things. I remember this questioning of my faith was extremely sketchy territory for me at the time.

After a few years of very gently looking around forbidden corners, I had slowly accepted that there was a lot more to life than I had been taught in Sunday School. It took many years for me to finally let go of some of my most *identity defining* beliefs. I was no longer following the straight and narrow path that had been laid out for me.

As a result, of my newly acquired and expanding awareness, I started to feel a real sense of urgency to learn as much from my Aunt as possible. I know that my Aunts health was waning fast and we had lots of work to do.

I lived in Dallas, Texas and she lived in Roswell, New Mexico, where I was born. A lot of my family still lives there. Most of our visits were over the phone, and we would often talk for hours, with my incessant flow of questions. Fortunately, I was able to visit her in Roswell two or three times a year for the last few years of her life. There was never a trip that I didn't get exactly what I needed to hear. In an unspoken awareness between my Aunt and myself, we both knew well what was happening; she was passing the torch.

As her teachings became more and more experiential for me, no longer just concepts, I began to better understand the subtleties of my transformation, as well as the implications of how truly amazing this process of life really was.

My Aunt Jane passed away a few years later and I missed her dearly. Even though she was gone physically, her essence and passion for life continued to manifest within me.

I had evolved through the old teachings and feelings of

separateness into a total experience of interconnectedness. I was now seeing how things worked. I had felt guided and protected for much of my life and could now *see* and *feel* this connection. I felt that all of the pieces of myself were genuinely integrating. My life experiences were now guiding me in a new direction.

With time and the reconciliation of a lifetime of seemingly unrelated personal miracles, I finally felt the connection… literally. As I began seeing things from a deeper perspective, I knew that there were way too many amazing things happening throughout my life for all of those things to be coincidences. I knew that my life had always felt guided. Winding up in the jewelry business was one of many examples of how we are nudged in one direction or another. The awareness needed to understand how or why these things were happening was slowly beginning to unfold.

Everything on this new path was making sense. It was even making sense of what never made sense before. I remember thinking that as long as all the dots were connecting, I would keep going down this ever-broadening path.

My Aunt Jane's spiritual lessons were distilled from a vast range of scripture and ancient texts. She used teachings from around the world, from indigenous traditions to early Christian roots. This universal collection of spiritual material contained a common thread that when pulled together, revealed the essence of life and creation. This common thread was oneness, not fear.

My great Aunts teachings were deeply engrained within my consciousness, but now, 15 years after my first spiritual inquisition, and at the age 45 years old, I was experiencing for the second time in my life an intense compulsion for an even higher spiritual understanding. This "pulling feeling" I was having would culminate in a series of experiences and revelations that I will explore a little later in this book.

After some life altering decisions to pursue this *pulling away* from my old life, I began to see that there was a new path emerging. Primed by the teachings of my Great Aunt and my growing compulsion for higher awareness, the student from within myself was now ready for the next chapter. The torch that my Great Aunt had passed on to me was calling loudly to be carried forward and passed onto others. I spent nearly the next ten years opening doors to a variety of experiences and dimensions that would eventually realign my view of reality.

One of the first emerging spiritual concepts was related to the inherent intelligence within every particle of energy. I was able to quantify through my personal experiences, that the root of absolutely everything is pure energy. In 1810, even before quantum mechanics had made its debut, Thomas Young performed an experiment that would ultimately challenge our finite understanding of the nature of energy. His experiment would be replicated many times over the next 200 years and still challenges the mechanistic view of life. His experiment is simply known as, *Thomas Young's double slit experiment.* I would encourage everyone to read the research.

It turns out, that energy can behave as a particle or as a wave. There seems to be an inherent intelligence capable of making choices as needed. Every particle of energy is completely capable of synchronistic behavior. Our interaction with energy, as an observer, or even as thought, triggers a cooperative response. Energy and matter are merely two aspects of one reality; Einstein proved that with his Theory of Relativity.

Science has evolved to the point, where even many of our native spiritual beliefs are validated through a quantum point of view. This synergistic relationship between energy and matter, in effect, also validates our connections with earth and spirit.

When we experience all of life as interconnected conscious energy, we experience one source. We are not our ego based bodies, we are of spirit, we are of energy, we are of the infinite; and the endless, incomprehensible mind of intelligent design, God, as the creative collective consciousness within all life.

Science may not give you the answer you were looking for, but looking for specific answers is not looking for the truth. When you see life through the eyes of spirit, you can clearly see that the energy we share is the life force itself. We are a physical form, but we are not our bodies. We are more than you can probably imagine at this point.

My search has taken me from Christianity into the study of Hindu philosophy, Buddhism, Taoism, Shamanism, Quantum Sciences, and even the psychic realm. When you look at the root of all of this information you will see that there is not only a pattern, there's an underlying common reality. This common reality is that we are all connected all the time, to each other, and to everything around us.

The evolution of consciousness is about freeing our minds. It's about living in full awareness that we are spiritual beings having a physical experience to complete our soul's chosen purpose. In doing this, we add perspective to the collective consciousness from which we came. This may not be what you were told by the powers that be, but I promise if you diligently seek the truth, you will find it. The quest is part of the process. The answers are all around us, all the time. We have only to open our consciousness to the idea that there may be something outside of our tiny little bubbles.

I know well what it's like to live within these little bubbles. I've lived within many. I've lived in a religious bubble that I was afraid to look out of, for fear of retribution. I've lived in a political bubble that made me feel safe and justified. I lived in a sociological bubble that made me feel successful and proud. These bubbles give us the illusion that we are protected in some way or are at least a part of something greater than ourselves. I eventually discovered that bubbles, like most beliefs, will burst when prodded deeply enough.

All of my beliefs were just that, beliefs. Beliefs are passed down through generations of conditioning. Our religion, political views and even sociological beliefs are very similar to that of our parents, as it is from theirs. We've been culturally conditioned to conform. Most families don't encourage non-conformity, so we fall in line. In essence, we've been set down our path; we didn't choose it.

Shedding dogmatic conditioning and behavior is part of the journey for the seeker of truth. It's important for us to look carefully at the things and beliefs that we often vehemently defend. Almost all wars are fought over one belief or another. Conformity and intolerance are potentially the world's greatest challenges.

There have been many significant experiences that have influenced me through my quest for higher consciousness. One that I will discuss next provides a clear picture of how the journey of life itself also provides the process for self-discovery. I will begin by telling you this next story because it contains all of the elements that best demonstrate how beautiful this life experience is when lived consciously.

Conscious awareness means that we have become conscious observers of our experiences. We learn how to recognize patterns that emerge and to follow our inner feelings as *guidance*, not out of fear. As we grow *through* each experience, we grow in consciousness, and this heightened awareness carries forward through eternity.

Part of our new awareness allows us to recognize and acknowledge new patterns in our life. These patterns are generally guideposts pointing towards a potential new path. Each conscious experience will always lead you to the next revelation. I'm sure as you read on you'll begin to identify with some of your own seemingly coincidental experiences and learn how things really do, "just work out."

I want to clarify something. This story of mine is not about what "I did" it's about what's going on within and around all of us, all the time. Our role in life is to pay attention to what shows up around us. Only then can we consciously choose our path.

Within the following experience I had received multiple, seemingly coincidental, but related messages; trusted and followed my feelings about them, then put forth the diligence required to move forward. I was then given confirmation of the purpose of my experience. From this experience forward, I began to consciously recognize many more emerging patterns and learned that absolutely every experience in life matters. There are no coincidences.

Not all of my experiences were as dramatic as this one, but each element here had played out synchronistically and with a definite purpose. The "coincidences" and adjusted directions throughout my life had mounted up and couldn't be played off as mere chance anymore. I believe that my quest to understand those events is what leads me to what happened next. This next set of experiences occurred over about a two-year period. From its conception to its completion, this experience demonstrates just how life unfolds as we consciously participate in the process.

Life is not random. Each choice in life makes a difference in what we experience. The following story is an example of how things *can* work if we pay attention. I've done my best to describe both the physical and emotional state of each experience.

YOGA?

I had been on my spiritual path for some time at this point and had acquired at least a modest amount of spiritual awareness through meditation and other means. I knew that there were few if any, real coincidences. I knew that one occurrence of something might or might not mean much. Two related occurrences might be pointing at something worth considering, and three related occurrences was a sure slap in the head to wake up and pay attention. What happened next was no coincidence. I was being pointed in a specific direction. I felt though, that this path that I was being drawn down to was not that clearly marked, or so I thought. My intuition urged me to keep looking down this road.

Here's the short version of what I call *"the yoga experience"* as it played out. This next series of events shows very well how each conscious choice along our path not only creates our next opportunity, it forms our eventual self.

I was visiting with a friend one afternoon when she very randomly said to me, *"you should try Yoga!"* Yeah, right! I thought to myself. I quickly dismissed the idea and changed the subject. Yoga was not anywhere on my radar.

Less than a week later another friend said the same thing, *"have you ever tried Yoga?* this was also out of the blue. I dismissed it again but acknowledged the coincidence. Within a few more days a total stranger that I was having a conversation with said, *"you should try Yoga!"* I smiled to myself and acknowledged that I needed to pay attention.

It was a few weeks later that I found myself pulling into a parking lot. I wasn't looking for anything, but there happened to be a Yoga studio just around the corner. I thought to myself; I guess this is where I'm supposed to be, so I went inside to talk to the woman about their programs. I don't remember all of my thoughts at the time, but something didn't seem quite right, and I wound up not going back. I didn't think much more about it.

There was another Yoga studio that I'd driven by many times but was never compelled to go in. Finally, one day I decided that I should check them out. It wasn't far from my house so I thought I'd just drop by. I pulled up to their building, but no one was there. I tried another time, and again, no one was there. Oh well, I thought. There still seemed nothing much to consider.

A couple of weeks later I saw someone leaving that Yoga studio, so I quickly pulled into the parking lot to check it out. Within just a few minutes of visiting with the Head Master, I knew that this was somehow a part of something I was being pointed towards. The studio wasn't fancy, but it felt very comfortable. There was a very warm and inviting feel about the place.

It turns out that this particular form of Yoga was not the, stick your foot behind your head kind of Yoga, it was a form of Korean Energy Yoga. The intent with this philosophy was to awaken dormant energy within the body to integrate your mind body and spirit. I hadn't experienced any of these techniques before, but I was intrigued and eager to broaden my perspective.

Before attending this form of Yoga, I'd had had a reasonable amount of meditation practice, spiritual study, and had worked intensely for several years with a physical trainer. My inadvertent preparation was going to make a big difference with this new form of training.

I was making great strides in this new program and moved quickly up the ranks. For those of us that were ready, and interested, they offered even higher levels of training. These higher levels dealt specifically with the transformational nature of energy and the higher dimensions of reality. These were not basic classes. Many students didn't partake in these classes for various reasons. Diligence in this energy work is what moved me, and some my classmates, to still higher levels of training.

Part of this higher training was in Austin, TX. These were programs designed specifically to challenge some of our most identity defining beliefs. It felt very much like a spiritual boot camp. There were specific programs designed to tear down and realign each self-imposed boundary. Like peeling away layers of an onion, we discovered more and more of our true nature. The point here was to exceed mental and physical barriers that we didn't even know existed. The intent was not to change us; it was to create the opportunity for us to experience our higher nature. This experience not only awakened dormant energy; it had also significantly broadened my spiritual awareness.

After completing these programs, some of us were offered even further training. They invited some of us into their healing programs and still more advanced training classes. We were also given the opportunity to meet the Head Master from Korea at another event in Austin. This was more a social event than training, but it was still an honor for all of us to meet this Master.

The next door to open for me was a healing session with the top healer within this global organization. This was something that they offered to me as a gift, and was part of an even higher experience, definitely not part of the routine. The Master would be visiting from Korea within a few weeks, and I had my private appointment set. The following experience would drastically affect my life again.

The Master and I started with a short visit to discuss the intent of the healing session and get acquainted. We had discussed aspects of my personal life and career, and I informed him that I felt that part of my true purpose was more spiritual in nature, but I wasn't sure how. We talked for a few more minutes and then we started our session.

It began with a form of moving mediation. The purpose of this meditation was simply to commit to the process as your body and mind align. Surprisingly, for meditation, the process was very physically demanding. The process started out standing, then kneeling, then stretching our arms far out in front with your face on the floor. We would then sit up and stand without using your hands and do it again. It took a little while to get the hang of it.

He and I did this together continuously for about an hour. The process soon became *very* emotional for me. I felt an extreme sense of gratitude throughout the process, to the point of tears. At the end of the process, we sat in silent meditation for about 15 minutes after which we spoke briefly again about the intent of the meditation. It was an amazingly beautiful experience, a true gift.

What I experienced next I can only explain as a bizarre, intense feeling of confusion and disbelief. In the precise moment that I stood up, it felt like an internal power cord had just been yanked out of my body; like an appliance cord being ripped from the wall. It was an abrupt, physical, disconnection. *I couldn't believe it!* I was stunned from the experience and could barely conceive of what had just happened. I had gone from a feeling of bliss and communion to a state of total disconnection and confusion in one instant. I spontaneously felt no connection at all to any part of the organization. I thought to myself, what the hell is going on!

Fortunately, I didn't live far away, so I left. I could barely focus on driving but did manage to make it safely back to my house. I had previously committed to attend one of the evening training classes at the Yoga Center, but now, I couldn't bring myself to go. One of the instructors and one of the other students called to check on me, but I couldn't bring myself to answer the phone. Something was seriously wrong. My internal compass was spinning out of control, and nothing about this experience made any sense.

I mulled about my house for a while to sort out what the hell was going on in my head. For some unknown reason, I got back in my car and started driving again with no destination in mind. I had no desire to go back to the yoga studio, yet I found myself back at the studio anyway. All of the Masters were in the parking lot getting ready to go home. I told two of the Masters that we needed to talk, but there seemed to be no connection between us at all. We'll talk tomorrow, they said. I thought that a walk around the neighborhood might help, so I decided to go back to the house.

I had just recently moved to this neighborhood and wasn't completely familiar with all of the streets. I picked a direction and started walking for about half a mile when I reached a point that I needed make a decision, to either go back the direction that I came or loop back around on a busier street. Because of my training up to this point, I felt intuitively that even the simple choice in what direction to go would somehow be an important one; I decided to take the loop around.

I was consciously taking in everything around me, to make some sense of what had just happened. As I turned the corner, I saw a very large lighted sign on the side of a building. It was the only sign that was visible to me at that moment. The sign read, "Entrust". It was just the name of the bank, but I felt somehow that it meant more than that given the gravity of the situation.

I kept walking in deep contemplation about what had just happened. I was still very aware of being in sort of a *Twilight Zone*. Spontaneously, I remembered a crazy thing that often happens to me while I'm in deep thought. Street lights will go out right when I get close to them. I don't mean a few times; I mean a hundred times or more throughout my life. It even happened on three consecutive lights, while I was in Albuquerque with my mother. These occurrences feel like guidance of some sort, but I've never completely understood their purpose. I feel that they may be just reminders that we are not alone in this experience.

Anyway, just as I'm having this thought about street lights going out and thinking to myself, this really is when one should go out, no kidding, within about two seconds, the street light right over my head went out. I wasn't surprised at all; it seemed just perfect. The word *Trust* was something I was supposed to pay attention to, but trust in what? Was I to trust my instincts or trust the process that I was going through or both? I kept walking and thinking about this *Trust* thing; what was I supposed to trust?

Within a few more minutes of walking down this street I saw another large lighted sign, again, the only sign visible to me at that moment. It was Northern Trust Bank, the word trust again! Normally, this bank sign wouldn't mean anything to anyone, but I knew this wasn't just *any time*. A big smile came over my face... *I get it*! Instantly, I was overcome with this *intense* sense of gratitude. *Trust in myself*!! This was the feeling that I was overcome with. Now guess what happened next? The street light I was now under just went out. *Now*, I was even more overwhelmed by the experience and broke into tears of gratitude.

As bizarre as it all seemed, I had just received a level of confirmation that cemented for me, a true knowing, that within my soul laid all the answers. I was not separate from anything except as a belief. This new awareness of my inner guidance gave me a total sense of completion and peace. I was experiencing my true nature and any remnant of the illusion of separateness vanished. I was experiencing the evolution of my spiritual awareness through my effort to see it.

Throughout life, our conscious experiences provide context for the answers that lie within each of us. Each life experience presents its opportunities, and it's our willingness to explore them that creates our reality.

The experience of the last two years had greatly broadened my perceptions of "Reality." I still had boundaries, but they stretched out a lot further.

My last experience with the healer was to be my last experience at the Yoga studio. I was given a not so subtle signal, "put in the time and effort to figure it out," and was given confirmation that my time with the Yoga studio was now over. I acknowledged that this abruptly odd end was necessary for me to separate and move forward, and to always trust in my inner guidance.

The last two years with the Yoga studio had impacted my life in ways that can barely be explained. The higher purpose of this experience was to learn to live consciously. I had also learned to better recognize emerging patterns as guideposts. If I hadn't acknowledged the seemingly random questions asked of me by three different people, "Have you ever thought about taking Yoga?" I wouldn't likely have taken that path. To me, this story is about seeking the truth, and always being open to new perspectives. Our growth comes from exploring the often-fragile outer edges of our perceived reality. The pain of prodding keeps many of us from going very deep. I encourage everyone to listen mindfully to their inner resistance. This process will likely open doors for you that you'll *eventually,* be glad that you did. Remember, a doorway passed, isn't missed, unless you're afraid to go back through it.

This new state of awareness had opened portals to other dimensions. One of the portals that opened was the portal of communication. By tuning our minds and bodies to a receptive frequency, we can open up various channels of awareness, and within this awareness, we experience our connection to the universal mind. I was now experiencing this connection.

Each time I would sit to meditate, I would be bombarded, with mostly cryptic messages that I felt compelled to write down. I had to stop meditating just to take notes. Even my sleep was interrupted by messages *drifting by*, or that's how it felt to me. Some were as thoughts, and some as voices, like someone was speaking in my left ear. At one point, I was sleeping with a notepad because the messages were so fleeting, that by the time I got up to write them down, they were gone. I was even writing in the dark just to capture the essence of some of the messages.

After compiling all of these random messages on pieces of paper, I finally read through some of these cryptic messages and decided that I needed to elaborate on these fragmented notes so that other people might eventually have some idea of what the original concept was. Most of the original messages were short statements while others rambled for pages.

I've tried to keep the integrity within all of the messages, while clarifying some concepts, for those just beginning their quest. It's not specifically important what you get from this; it's only important that you start your individual process of exploration.

Some of the messages can be traced back for thousands of years in various forms. Some of the messages may seem familiar as they speak of universal principals, while others address troubling social issues. These messages came to me with a crystal-clear understanding of the principles behind the words. This book is my attempt to share their meaning through my experiences.

I have visually seen the movement of energy within

inanimate objects and experienced energy at work in a multitude of ways. If you look diligently enough, you will discover what's real. You will see through the illusions around you. My hope is that there is something here that sparks your curiosity. This is only a guidepost, and each of us must choose our path.

I can only give you a tiny glimpse into the realities that I've experienced. I can't call them a specific reality, but I can call them my diligent effort to view what's around the proverbial corner. I promise you, once you open your heart, you'll experience the answers that you seek.

Seek first the Kingdom, and then listen. This commitment to *Listen* will be your first conscious choice toward enlightenment. Quiet your mind and breathe deeply this simple word: *Listen.* Then just listen!

It's been said that life is a gift that many leave unopened. It's time to open yours. Question everything, but *feel* and express intense gratitude for everything. Start where you are now, right now, and as your gratitude grows, a broader awareness will follow. This is when your opportunities will begin manifest. Each step builds on the last. There is no destination in play here, only the process of self-realization. As you read on you'll see why.

Man's original sin was the illusion of separateness.
The moment we lost sight of our higher self,
we walked blindly alone.

Part of the purpose of this book is to dispel the illusion of separateness. We are spiritual beings connected to nature in a way that we may not be able to imagine. Our connection to universal energy has been forgotten. Our job here through this life is to experience the manifestation of this connection through our renewed awareness. This rebirth, is our salvation into a consciously lived life.

THE DEEPER MEANING

The Tao Te Ching is a twenty-five-hundred-year-old beautifully simple philosophy for living. One of its basic tenant's states very concisely: "The name that can be named is not the eternal name." To me, what he's saying is, that as long as we only recognize the surface level interaction of something, we'll be substantially limited in our understanding of it. Part of our higher purpose here is to live as consciously aware as possible, to better interpret the evolving nature around us. To do this, we must first acknowledge that there is a much deeper reality to experience. Once we begin to experience this deeper nature, we will begin to feel the deeper connection that exists within all life.

This is why it's vitally important to always seek the higher meaning behind any message. This book contains a lot of information that, if not embodied to its deepest level, won't mean that much either. This book is about expanding your awareness, and seeing life from your own unique and evolving conscious perspective. We should always seek to embody the essence of any message, and not just mimic the words that we see and hear.

As we begin to embody the truth around us, we will begin to better see our true nature. This is when our intended purpose begins to emerge and develop. Your evolving purpose will mold your new awareness. Your new awareness will yield new beliefs.

Our beliefs are the basis for how and what we do. Our

beliefs and our awareness should forever be evolving. As we become more aware, our beliefs will expand. This evolving consciousness will change your life and your perception of everything. You can be no more or no less than what you believe. Your beliefs are your boundaries, and only you set the limits. In essence, this book is a journey in consciousness. It's my hope that as you seek the deepest meaning behind the words in this book and discover the deepest parts of yourself. Remember that this book is also about self-discovery; it's not about looking for specific answers. The truth is not in what you read; it is in what you discover about yourself.

During this inquisition into my soul, I can't say that I lost my faith. What I feel is that I found the truth...

We will have discovered our true selves when we can see that through the infinite paths we take, and with each new thread of discovery, we weave the fabric of life itself. The pattern you create is up to you.

The Gift of You

When the sounds of silence are no longer peaceful and light, and your soul feels hard... tired... and weak. Seek then to give to another what you think you have lost. Give love, compassion, and tenderness to someone in need. It's the gift of you that the world so desperately needs.

MOVING FORWARD

Through my personal quest I have taken many steps forward, but now I find myself now taking a few steps back. I fully accept the implications of the interconnectedness of everything. I accept that each dimension co-exists through vibrational frequencies. I accept that consciousness transcends dimensions. I also accept that my understanding is only as it is for now, and that our intended progress is through the incarnation of our evolving spirit. More than anything, I see that the primary function of this life experience is not to try to get to a better place or communicate with other dimensions. Our purpose is to consciously seek our potential and live it. Each of us has so many hidden gifts and talents, and part of our purpose here is to help one another find these gifts, through our interactions and relationships. It's only through the contrast of our experiences, that it's possible to discover who we are.

We are part of a dynamically active interconnected universe, and we are also a unique conscious aspect of it. Universal awareness is expanded through each expression of life. We exist as conscious energy in both finite and infinite realities. Through these experiences, all things evolve. We have infinite opportunities to consciously evolve. Until we do, we are destined to live out countless lifetimes of misery and discontent.

In order to move forward through incarnations, we must acknowledge that we have a purpose within this life experience. This purpose is to understand we are spiritual beings in a physical experience. The purpose of the physical body is to experience contrast. We cannot grow spiritually, or experientially, without the experience itself. Our task is to understand fully that we are spiritual beings with a purpose. As physical beings, we must fully accept our role as humans. Our higher purpose is to integrate these plains of consciousness, or there will be no appreciable growth without it. If we live out our physical existence, without spiritual growth, then we stay stagnant in consciousness. Our spiritual and physical growth is dependent on our ability to embody our higher consciousness while fulfilling our physical lives. Spiritual awareness is not about retreating from responsibility; it's learning to fully integrate our spiritual self into our daily lives. This integration requires full acknowledgment of your higher self and its interconnected nature. We cannot accept a "once a week" approach to spirituality. We must experience ourselves as the spiritual beings that we are. To accomplish this, we have to strive towards balance. We must develop a mindfulness that never loses sight of our spiritual connection or our physical requirements. All of our actions become inspired by spirit.

Daily meditations are a great first step towards a solid foundation of higher awareness. Hopefully, in a short time, you'll be able to embody your spiritual essence, moment by moment, while impacting the world in your own unique way. We are spiritual beings evolving through consciousness. All of this not only takes practice, it takes commitment. This commitment is not out of commandment, but out of your desire to experience your higher self. Contrary to what we may have been told, spiritual growth requires taking responsibility for yourself. Fortunately, everything that you need is within you already. Your salvation lies within your desire to experience it. As you seek, you will find.

As we grow consciously, we begin to gravitate to higher plains, and start to recognize the signs of internal change. This internal awareness is ultimately what guides your choices and direction. The more self-aware that we become, the more confident we become with our feelings and choices.

This internal awareness is like a compass and must be calibrated accurately for it to guide us. Calibration comes through living outside of the box, and discovering that your old fears were not true directions. This is an ongoing process. These misguided fears are the primary reason that your internal compass has led you in the wrong direction. Most people acknowledge their feelings, but the reason that many people don't trust their feelings is that these feelings have failed them too many times.

When fear has fogged your compass, it's difficult to see a clear direction. Fear creates an environment that is most likely to confuse your internal feeling about some decision. When you learn to distinguish how fear influences your decisions, you'll see that when you acknowledge and release these fears, your compass will lead you exactly where you need to go. Understanding the source of your fears is vital to your growth. As we evolve in consciousness, we move more quickly towards our purpose, throughout lifetimes. This is why prodigies move quickly into their fields of purpose. As you're seeking your purpose, be diligent and be patient. It may happen in an instant, or it may take a lifetime. Either path is worth the effort and will reward you in many ways throughout eternity. There's no single way to find your path. In fact, through your refined higher awareness, your purpose will most likely find you. This brings us back to my experience with the Yoga studio. It was through my persistent search for answers that the answer was given: To TRUST.

We must first develop an absolute trust in ourselves and understand that guidance is everywhere. We must trust that we are drawn to what resonates within us most. We must trust that in inherent laws of the universe act without exception. As we become more attuned with our higher self, our choices become more certain. We begin to sense the embedded purpose within each experience on our path. We begin to attract new opportunities and to experience them in new ways. Everything around us takes on a new significance and value.

As we acknowledge our refined feelings, we'll create a higher vibration of energy in that direction. These stronger signals are received and are energetically compelled to respond. It's called the law of attraction. These opportunities are produced by the acknowledgment of your passion and thus allow you to experience what excites you. This is how your purpose finds you. This is not a passive process. You have to become an active part of this process. The more energy that you put into your passion, the sooner you will realize you're potential. For those who say that they don't really have a passion, that's a little different approach. I believe that a life without a passion is a life short on love.

Within many people, there is a stifling lack of self-worth and self-love. To grow spiritually or emotionally, we must find a way to unconditionally love ourselves first. Love is the catalyst for growth.

We have to learn to let go of the stagnant memories that cause us pain and then tap into our higher self that sees through the pain. These bodies of ours have been through some tough times. It's our higher self, not the victim, which sees us through these experiences, to their higher purpose. It will take time and commitment to find your lost self. This is part of the process. We have only temporarily forgotten who we are. You will find yourself again, and you will love yourself again.

Through our newfound love of self, we will begin to feel again. Our passions will begin to take form. As your love strengthens, your passions will grow. Not only will your life change, you will begin to impact the lives of others as well; this is how life evolves. A life lived for the good of all is a good life indeed.

Thank you again for sharing this journey with me.

Remember that all of life is an opportunity to love, and when love guides your compass, everyplace is your home. Welcome home, and welcome to your new life!

The rest of this book is *not* intended to be read as you would normally read a book. There are no chapters. This book is a compilation of my experiences, thoughts, and revelations that are intended to evoke your dormant feelings or thoughts. The intention here is to present ideas that you may not have considered, or at least considered in the same way. Each of the following statements or messages is intended to plant a seed of curiosity. The purpose here is to challenge your inner student.; hopefully, you'll have far more questions that we can answer. When your inner student is truly ready, your journey will begin, and your consciously lived life will be a gift to everyone.

Please follow us online for methods and tools to help in your journey. Keep your attention on your goals, and never stop believing in yourself. Curiosity is the first step, so always dig a little deeper.

Feel free to read the rest of this book randomly. Just open to a page, feel its relevance at that moment. To discover yourself, you have to trust in yourself, and then love yourself deeply.

I hope you enjoy the process. Thank you again for this opportunity to share.

The face in the mirror, invisible to me...

is the truth seeking form, waiting to be.
For without this quest, for its life to see...
the truth into form, it Cannot be.

Life is all about balance, and how we balance change with tradition, and balance wisdom with innocence. Each moment that we exist, we must seek balance in our choices; this is both our challenge, and our opportunity in life.

PUZZLE PIECES

Regarding puzzle pieces made of puzzle pieces. A puzzle piece and be physical activity or even a big decision. The physiological aspect of the experience is another piece. The spiritual purpose and implications are the third aspect of the same piece of the puzzle. This example shows how we are continuously operating on multiple levels of potential awareness. It's not until all elements of each puzzle piece are fully considered and integrated that we fully grasp the implication and opportunities within each experience.

EACH PIECE MATTERS

If we look at all of life's experiences as puzzle pieces, then we wouldn't be so quick to dismiss or disregard the value of each experience. Each piece of the puzzle is important to the better understanding of the big picture. Each experience contains an embedded message. We must remember, any new piece of information we've discovered will not likely be fully recognized as what it really is, nor are we likely to understand all of its intricate implications. These new puzzle pieces will still be processed through our old filters of perception. For this reason, we must be very careful not to place too much face value on this new information. We must be clear as to exactly where this new information fits into our evolving paradigm. Without a thorough understanding of the interrelation of all experiences, you may misinterpret the purpose of that piece of information altogether.

Sometimes messages are so different from what we expect; we don't see them at all. When you have enough accumulated experiences, i.e. pieces of the puzzle, you'll have a much better idea of what the big picture is about. Just as with a real puzzle, the more of the pieces that you have together, the faster the rest of the pieces come together. The moral to this analogy is that the more consciously we experience life, the more pieces we collect, and the bigger the picture gets. As we see more and more, we will understand more and more. All you have to do is start looking for the pieces.

CHANGE

Change is a reality and an absolute within our lives. Everything around us changes in some way all the time. Some things may appear to be unchanged, but the rate of change is only slower than our perception. A rock may not seem to change, but over time it will take many forms. The way we look at change is what affects the way we experience life. We can experience change as the fear of the unknown, or, we can experience change as an exciting opportunity to create a new experience. Change can be something that you see happening to you, or change can be the conscious creation of a new vision.

These are obviously drastically different points of view, but my point here is that each point of view is a choice. It may not seem like a choice to you because of your existing beliefs; the reality is that you only believe what you believe, because you haven't considered, why you believe what you believe. We all have the tendency to think, that what we think, is the way that it should be. When you stop and consider honestly about why you believe what you do, you will realize that almost everything is in life is relative. Meaning, things only seem the way they do because of the way we think of them or in what context they are experienced.

What I'm getting at here is that change, and your belief about change, are forever intertwined. The only thing keeping you from the experience that you want, or what you think you want, is your belief, and how you view change.

Active change is when you begin to accept your role as the creator of your life. This is the beginning of your "real life." Through your evolving self-awareness, you begin to see why things are the way they are and begin to create your life with renewed enthusiasm.

Until you learn to transcend your resistance to change, you'll be operating out of what I call "reactive change." Reactive change is the birth place our "victim" mentality, it's when life is happening to us. If we're just reacting to life's circumstances, then we wind up being part of someone else's vision and feel out of control. You have to, very consciously, create your life to fulfill your higher intended purpose. Once you accept that change is how we evolve, you can rejoice in the knowing that it was only your belief about change that held you back. Now you can embrace your new life.

Between fear and faith, lie the angels that guide us. It's the whisper out of the silence, and the glimmer out of the darkness that shows us we have hope. When we look deep in the heart of this new sense of hope, we begin to feel our way through where we only stumbled before. We know where to move without the reason why. Our faith creates motion where fear held us down.

As Angels, we are all strands in this fabric of life. It's through compassion that we see ourselves as the stranger in need... as the giver, and the receiver. When we realize that we are truly part of the same fabric, we can clearly see that a tear in one piece is a tear in the whole. So we seek to mend... As we give to another, we heal one's self. As we love our self, we heal another. As we give of ourselves, we give hope. When we create hope for another, we become Angels.

What have you done to earn your wings today?

FEAR TO UNCERTAINTY, THE NEXT LOGICAL STEP

Fear is like an anchor... it leaves you firmly planted in the situation you're in, unable to move. Fear is also like a vice... squeezing so hard you can hardly breathe. If you can't move and can't breathe, then it's almost impossible to think clearly. You must first understand that almost all fear is an illusion and is self-created. It's based on an old belief system that has put you where you may be now... stuck in fear.

If we can pull up the anchor, i.e. take a chance, then we can at least move around a bit. Metaphorically, it's now a bit more like a ball and chain. We can get around, but it's still difficult. I relate the ball and chain metaphor to the feeling of uncertainty. When you're uncertain, you can still make progress but at a slower pace; fear to uncertainty seems like the next logical step. It's hard to go from fear, to no fear, without at least one step of uncertainty.

When you're willing to take that first step of uncertainty, you have just taken the first step out of that self-imposed box. As you begin to step out of your comfort zone, you'll soon experience the fact that all progress begins with that first uncertain step. Each new experience will represent exciting new opportunities for you. Each new step will bring joy instead of anxiety. Pull up the anchor and start moving.

We all have individual moments of clarity, but collectively we create the vision and the means to fulfill our journey.

The lesson itself can be the master when the student is ready...

THE MATRIX

The Matrix is whatever traps you. Our minds bring to life our vision of reality. That imposed reality is your "Matrix," your trap. Until you're aware that there is something outside the Matrix, you'll never even know to look. The clues that there is something else are all around us, yet we accept life for what we currently understand.

One day, in one moment, you may see or hear something that sparks a glimmer of curiosity. That curiosity can become a journey. Curiosity is the only requirement for awareness. Each step taken will open another door. Each door opened will expand your view of reality. There is no destination on the journey, only new awareness. Awareness is the basis for conscious creation. Awareness is the road out of your Matrix.

The great gifts of the world are not made; they are discovered. They exist within us as part of the universe. We can speak a truth, but we are not the creator of the truth. Once you become aware of the truth, you can share the truth. The spoken truth is only a window to the truth. One must open the window to experience the truth. Then, the light will truly shine in.

NOW

The power of being in this moment is that it gives you space. It lets you slow down the frantic exterior perception, and gives you a moment to consider a new perspective. It also allows you to create from within, instead of reacting to your environment. *Now*, is a moment of reflection and creation... *Now*, gives you the opportunity to step back from yourself and your situation and be the observer, not the reactor.

One of the first steps of being in the moment, is being open. You must first realize that your life is completely relative. That means that we each create our own realities moment by moment. When we become conscious of our ability to alter our own thoughts, we can eventually see that we've created our entire environment, including all of our relationships. We are where we are in life because of every decision we have made up to this point. When we learn to calibrate our perceptions, we can begin to consciously envision new realities. Within this and every moment is our choice. Be still and know...

It is as it is, and it is as it's not,

It's why you get what you fear
and not what you want.
When you stay in the light
and your intentions are clear,
the passions of life are what you hold dear.
So feel in your heart, the life that you choose,
because NOW is the moment,
and only your fear to lose.

I Know Who's in Charge!

So you say, "I make my own decisions"... "I have the final say." Unless you operate at a high level of self-awareness, which includes multiple dimensions, your decisions are likely being induced by a series of perceptions, most of which are very one-dimensional and biased. The decisions that most people make are processed through our personality filters, via our past experiences. These filters are so subjective and one dimensional that the primary decision maker in your "self" is the ego, not your conscious awareness.

This subconscious aspect of yourself is influenced by an infinite number of energies that you're constantly bombarded by.

Remember, all energy is connected and interacts with everything and everyone on some level. It doesn't matter whether they're across the room, or on the other side of the planet.

Most people cannot feel the energy around them; they're not tuned into it. To the unconscious mind, this random energy is the primary source of our feelings, and ultimately our decisions. We're not consciously self-aware enough to discern why we feel the way that we do; we just react.

In this model, you are very much like the boat going down the river without a paddle. You're just reacting to the energy around you. This is why most people feel out of control. They haven't remembered that to steer one's own life, they have to pick up the paddle and row. Being consciously self-aware gives you a better perspective of where you are, what you are doing, and what part of you is doing the thinking, and why.

EMPOWERMENT

True empowerment comes from the realization that everything is temporary. Once we realize that everything is in a constant state of creation, we can begin to create and appreciate all the beauty and grace around us. We must release the notion that there is some time in the future, whether it is a time, place or achievement that will bring us that final level of happiness. Even that seemingly steady job or business is subject to an abrupt end.

I'm sure that everyone in the world trade center on 9/11 was confident that their world was pretty predictable. It's these major events, and the precious moments, that forever provide the canvas for our lives. It's how we live each experience that is most important. We all have a lot to teach, and we all have a lot to learn. This is what makes each of us a part of each other.

Even though we seem to be individuals, we are indivisible. We are all one great creation, experiencing life from different points of view. Like the rays of the sun beaming in all directions, each having a unique experience. Some of the rays will help warm our planet and create the opportunity for our experience. Some rays will beam towards other planets, and still, other rays will travel for millions of light years across the universe. It's all one source, with infinite experiences, expressed through the individual experience, of every part of the whole.

The same scenario is true in every other aspect of our universe. From the largest planets and stars to the smallest particles known, we are all a part of creation in an inseparable way. When we realize our connection to everyone and everything, we can then begin to appreciate the scope of our journey. We will no longer feel alone or live in fear while hoping to re-join our source.

Our source is constant in its course of creation, yet ever changing in its expression of life. We are all a part of that expression of life, living, creating and experiencing through our eyes, as Gods' eyes. For me, this is true empowerment. The absolute knowing that there is no separation ever, between our source and ourselves. We are gifted with the opportunity to create at will, all of the wonders of the world. When Jesus states "these things and more ye shall also do," he is pointing out that creation is our gift, it is who we are.

OUR WILL

The universe doesn't contain good things and bad things…
just things, and potential things, as energy. All of this energy
and potential energy create a balance. Thoughts create
harmonious wave patterns that impact energy and move
potential energy into matter, through will. Don't laugh… The
movie, The Green Lantern demonstrates this very clearly. This
mode of creation is not fiction. The manifestation of matter
through will is demonstrated throughout history, and
throughout many ancient teachings.

The more intense and focused the thought and wave
patterns are, the more impactful they are. Intent always
precedes action, and everything we see, and even what we
can't see, is the result of intent on some level. Energy follows
intent. Intent moves energy through both subconscious space,
and our conscious and collective minds, and our will applies
the momentum and focus. Since all energy is connected, the
collective conscious and collective subconscious is always
creating the world we see around us. "We are both the child of
creation, and the mother creator of our world through intent
and will."

OUR SUBCONSCIOUS

Your subconscious mind is the program that runs your seemingly, conscious actions. You may think that you are making conscious decisions, but it's your subconscious beliefs that cause the neurons in your brain to react, thus creating your reality.

These beliefs are the building blocks that form our character. Our conscious thoughts just reinforce our beliefs, and therefore reinforce the neurological connections. When we're not in control of our thoughts, we become controlled by our thoughts. Once we take a step back and realize that we create our thoughts and that our thoughts are formed by our beliefs, then we can see how to consciously create our life. This may sound odd, but we can't just believe everything that we think. We must question why we think what we think.

Generally speaking, our thoughts are pre-conditioned. If you honestly think about this, you'll see that this is true. We have been pre-conditioned by everything we've ever experienced in life. Conscious thought requires a combination of projecting, reflecting, and understanding the present moment. I believe one has to clearly understand the present moment to clearly see where you've been, and where you want to go. This is where balance is required. I will often think back to a previous event to learn more from that experience. If we're frequently reviewing the past in a conscious effort to learn from it, then you can see how to more consciously create your new future. You can learn to create new realities through expanding your consciousness and developing broader perspectives. When you can clearly see the purpose of the past, you can more purposefully create any future you desire.

LOVE

A life void of love is a shallow existence in time. We *can* exist without love in our heart, but to truly experience life, we must experience love. To experience love, we have to open our heart without the fear of loss. Fear will poison any chance for real love. Without an open heart, there will always be a dark corner in our soul waiting for the light.

The Real You

We are one in spirit, unique in mind, with a purpose of expression and remembrance. We are the eyes, ears, and the touch of God as we create our experiences. As we remember our truly divine nature, we see hardships as our greatest gifts. We see not only the silver linings but also the golden heart that heals through our growth. When we see life through compassionate eyes, we begin to truly live. The real you is everywhere and in everything expressing itself as life.

ENERGY

We are surrounded by waves of energy all the time. We usually don't recognize or feel this energy. It can be in the form of radio waves, television signals, human vibrations, essentially anything. These pervasive energy waves are all received through our subconscious mind. It's like receiving subliminal advertising 24/7.

Your subconscious mind doesn't discriminate; it just stores this energy as information. These pervasive waves of information influence your mental operating system just like downloaded software. Until we learn to filter and manage this data, we become programmed by it. Your mind can only process what it has to work with. It's up to us to manage what goes in so that we can control what comes out. This is the first step in becoming self-aware and taking responsibility for our decisions. As we learn to manage our thoughts we can begin to gain control of our lives. Random energy is no longer programming our realities.

Your belief is your prison. Curiosity is the key out.

Our finite perception of reality is the illusion.
Our imagination is the only limitation.

Perspective

There are multiple levels of perspectives within any situation. Here's an example: You have your physical, seemingly "conscious" reality. Then you have the subconscious reason for creating that reality. Then you have the higher spiritual purpose within that reality.

I'll be more specific... Let's say that on the "conscious" day-to-day level; you're afraid to speak in public. Your subconscious might be telling you that you're not worthy or not smart enough; this is a trigger for you. This whole scenario is likely set up by you on the spiritual level to give you the opportunity to overcome your fears.

We create our reality by recognizing the truth about ourselves. When we realize that we are spiritual beings creating physical realities through our imagination, we begin to awaken. You can now create out of a sense of purpose because you're following your purpose. This, you will feel, in your entire body.

Ask yourself this: Are you just getting through this life while waiting to get to a better place? Or can you see yourself as a soul with a purpose that's connected to everything? They will be completely different lives, and both by choice. Both serving a higher spiritual purpose, whether or not the actions are conscious or not. All experiences count as experiences, and each one builds on the last. You won't be presented something that you can't handle. If you are, you will most likely lose it and have to chalk it up to experience.

A wise person will accept this. He will accept that he wasn't ready for the experience and look to grow from the experience. Many will make an excuse or point the finger of blame. It's hard for most people to accept total accountability for their lives. Accountability means responsibility, and that means action and change. Changing one's actions requires conscious effort, and that implies an acknowledgment that there needs to be a change. Change only happens when someone is tired of suffering. Life is a process of learning that we don't have to suffer. The easiest way to find yourself is just to be yourself, and pay attention to what moves and excites you, then be the work that you love to do.

In an unconscious life, it takes the pain of the present moment to be greater than the pain of the unknown, for change to occur.

If you don't have a balanced approach, you most certainly have a biased approach.

Belief requires subjugation, Creation is limitless.

Remember, observations are merely our judgments about what is being perceived, and our perception is influenced by our own past experiences. It's a shame that so many people suffer because of their perception or point of view. Even a slight shift in perception can change the entire world.

You become who you are by thinking about what you are. Each decision that you make will give you a glimpse into your true self-worth. When you upgrade the thoughts of what you are, then you will ultimately become who you want to be.

Each time you surprise yourself, you're creating a new footstep out of the box. Don't be too surprised when you find the box has lost its purpose. Instead of living inside the box you can stand on it and get a clearer vision of where and who you want to be. Think big and take even bigger steps.

BUBBLES

When you can step out of your bubble and see that there are an infinite number of bubbles, you can clearly see that each bubble is just a choice. We create our lives by combining these bubbles of experience in any way we choose. Each decision creates change, and each decision creates you. The point here is to live among and acknowledge each bubble of experience, but not be trapped or identified by them. As the Masters have told us, our challenge is to live in this world but not be consumed or identified by it.

We must realize that our perception creates our reality, and our understanding sets the boundaries. When we can see that new awareness sets new boundaries, then the limits we perceive can no longer deceive us.

THIS LANGUAGE WE LIVE

The spiritual world operates through a unique language of its own. Many people can speak the words and herald their truth, but few see, feel, and grasp the powerful implications that live within this language.

True spirituality is not about words; it's about the experience within the words. This is a great example of having to be ready to hear the words, in order to live them. If there's not a reasonable foundation for understanding first, then the words will just pass along a story. When there is a stable foundation of understanding, the words create an emotional experience.

There will ultimately be a moment of immense clarity when the words that you've been reading or listening to become visions in your mind, and emotions that beckon your soul. This is when the spiritual language transcends the words. This is when you begin living from this new sense of awareness and your dreams take on an entirely new purpose. You'll begin to genuinely feel your connection with everyone and everything. It will be as if everything up to this point was a dream. The reality is, it was a part of a dream, a dream that you are alone and have to prove something to survive. The illusion that you are separated from your source is the primary cause of emotional pain. You are not separate from anything.

As you continue your quest, you'll begin to experience the

words that guide you, and the pain of frustration will turn to joy and immense gratitude. Gratitude is the seed that unfolds to bear the fruit of love. This seed is our gift through awareness. When we truly understand this spiritual language we live, we know that we are love. We are the actual material manifestation of compassion, as love. This cannot be taken away.

Within each and every experience is an opportunity for introspection and self-evaluation. Impress yourself with what you see.

Life doesn't flourish because it's afraid not to. Life is created through a balancing of energy and awareness through an innate cooperative effort. Life in this way is a gift of creation, not a threat of compliance. Nothing is created through fear, except followers.

TIME TO GROW

The only reason not to be living the life of your dreams is that you haven't figured out what life you want yet. Any other reason is probably an excuse. We've all come up with lots of reasons why we can't or aren't doing what we really love. We've been programmed to do this our whole life. This is just part of the group mentality. I'm not saying that groups are bad, they aren't. There are millions of groups/institutions that do wonderful things in many ways.

What I'm saying is that all groups have a group identity, a group agenda. A group can be a family, business, a church, or whatever. As part of a group, we help support the rest of the group, by re-affirming the group agenda. This means that it's our role as an individual, to help support the structure of the whole by confirming the mantras that keep the group, a group. Some of the mantras are; I have responsibilities, so I have to… It would be selfish for me to… It's not safe to…

These, and many other statements like these, infer an obligation of alliance to the group. I'm not saying that you have to leave your family or quit your job or take great risk to pursue your personal development. This is your life were talking about.

What I'm trying to convey is that your group will most likely resist your desire to significantly change something that affects them. Your desire to pursue your higher self, has to exceed your fear of their criticism. When people start looking outside the traditional box, it makes everyone in the box a little uneasy. This is why when you start talking about your dreams you'll begin to hear the group mantras telling you to, "Come back to reality" or "You can't do that!" That's why it's best to keep your dreams to yourself until you've developed a good foothold in that direction.

Until you have chosen your direction, and have already taken the first steps, the group will try to bring you back or rattle your cage. Remember that the group is made up of individuals, and most of your group will be family and friends. For the most part, these are the first people that will throw water on your passionate ideas, or tell you to "get real." Remember… "real" for most people means safe. This doesn't make them wrong and you right, it just means that any real growth requires a bigger box, a little imagination.

WE ONCE BELIEVED

It used to be we believed what we believed because that's all that we could see. We believed the earth was flat because it looked flat. It seemed like the sun revolved around the earth, so it was logical at that time to assume that the earth was the center of everything. Today the Hubble and Kepler telescopes have allowed us to peer millions of light years into the heavens, and our electron microscopes and supercolliders, take us in the quantum world where pure energy lives.

If we can believe what we can see, then the world we live in is only limited by one thing, and that one thing is our imagination. We have to broaden our imagination to grasp the implications of what we can actually see. Our human eye hasn't yet caught up with what our mind's eye is capable of seeing. Today we can see things that we've never seen before, but until we can understand what we're looking at, we will still be making up stories to try to make sense of the past. The stories of man, and the stories of science should only be considered snapshots of what we understand today. We should always seek to know more about ourselves. The only way to do that is by always trying to look further around each corner.

One paradox about believing what you see is that you can't always believe what you see. Often, things presented as facts can be attempts to advance a particular agenda. This is why we should question what we've been taught as, Reality. Not out of trying to salvage an old belief, but out of due diligence for good information.

Here's another fly in the ointment of believing what you see. The vast majority of what is happening around us can't be seen. The energy that is creating everything around us, including our experiences, cannot be seen; this is where you have to rely on your feelings, your instincts, and the results that you see around you. You may not see the energy move between people in love, but you can certainly experience it.

Energy is everywhere all the time; it is the only reason that anything happens. Only when there is an exchange of energy does something happen. It takes energy to make a thought. Thoughts move energy, and as energy moves, it creates. Moving energy ultimately creates more and more mass. Mass uses and creates more energy. The process of creating never stops. What we know today is a paradigm shift away from what we knew only one lifetime ago. Imagine what tomorrow will bring!

Happiness lies not with the modest or the meek, nor the rich and powerful. Happiness is simple in the mind that accepts the gift.

Until you're seeking something, you're not likely to find anything. This is why most of life's treasures go unnoticed. When you seek the kingdom, the universe will answer.

Whatever we give power to, becomes our Savior.

ENTANGLEMENT

Maybe, the best way to understand spirituality is by comparing how astronomers use different frequencies of telescopes to see distant stars and galaxies. Telescopes can collect data from various spectrums, then compile the data to create multi-dimensional projections of an object. To see anything with limited dimension gives you almost no idea of what you're looking at. To fully understand the entanglement of energy and spirituality, you have to experience it from multiple dimensions. The purpose of your spiritual path is to show you doors you've been forbidden to open. Once you pass through, you can never un-see the truth.

GOD

Stephen Hawking has taken us from superstition to a quantifiable explanation of the origin of the universe. He believes that there is no need for a god because science has evolved to the point where there is solid science, using the basic laws of the universe, like gravity and the quantum behavior of energy, to simply explain the cause and effect of creation. I believe though, what he has left out are the principals and implications of energy and its inherent consciousness.

Mankind not only has conscious awareness, but all matter has its own level of conscious awareness Our consciousness is interconnected with universal energy at all times. It's through this interconnectedness that there becomes, what we call, the collective consciousness. This collective consciousness contains all of the information that has ever existed. My contention is not only do we have access to this awareness, but this collective consciousness is also self-aware.

This collective evolves as we do. We connect with each other through this connection, and we connect to dimensions beyond our own. Everything is available to everyone depending on your vibrational awareness. This is the infinite evolution of consciousness.

To me, this interconnected, self-aware, evolving state of consciousness is God. As we evolve, God evolves, and as God evolves, we evolve. This is how thoughts create matter and how minds create miracles. When one's individual consciousness is in harmony with divine nature, anything is possible.

Heaven and hell are states of consciousness
that travel with us eternally.

The Why of It

When looking at why things are the way they are, it's not about explaining it from the religious perspective or the scientific perspective. It's about understanding the spiritual connection that brings everything together. It's about understanding the universal principles that apply to everything. Once we understand the underlying nature of how the physical and the nonphysical interact, we can then begin to understand the relative nature of our physical and spiritual experiences.

EVOLUTION

Evolution is the manifestation of an evolving consciousness. Someone asked, "How does consciousness evolve from matter?" The answer is that consciousness and matter exist symbiotically. Consciousness and matter are eternally evolving together. Matter, the physical expression of evolution, exists within our physical dimension. Consciousness, which is a part of our spiritual evolution, transcends dimensions. When we talk about consciousness, we have to understand that there are many levels of consciousness, just as there are infinite forms of matter. Matter exists in the form of particles and consciousness exists as waves of potential. All matter has some inherent consciousness, i.e. Intelligence. Consciousness is forever evolving and intertwined through all matter. Matter and consciousness are as synonymous, as are mass and energy. Consciousness exists within all energy at some level. Machines are engineered matter. Even engineered intelligence evolves in consciousness. Eventually, consciousness evolves into self-awareness. Consciousness is an inherent part of nature. Consciousness is not bestowed upon us; it evolves within us. Consciousness is our true form; it is who we are, and how we exist eternally. Our bodies are simply the manifestation of our Will for the physical experience through consciousness expression.

It's only through our relationships that we can experience the relative nature of things. Relationships create the opportunity to experience life from a different perspective if you're aware enough to look for it. Our nature is relative, but our life is absolute. We exist relatively throughout our existence in life.

CYCLES OF REALITIES

In an infinite reality, your mind makes whatever dimension you're in seem real. I'm sure most of you have had dreams that you would have sworn were real. Just like in a dream you never lose your sense of self; you just change realities. Within an infinite cycle of Realities, we experience our relative world, and then back to a metaphysical reality, over and over, until we choose otherwise. Each experience embodies a different objective until we complete our soul's purpose. When were finished in the relative world, we continue to evolve though your metaphysical self.

Your pure essence is always intact. You move at the speed of thought as a projected individual. As you free your mind, you will begin to move in infinite ways, always creating as you go. Doing is creating, and all thought is creating the next doing. You are never, not creating. All shifts in consciousness simultaneously create a ripple effect. Everything affects everything. By raising our personal awareness, we elevate the collective. We raise the universal consciousness every time we share our perspective.

To the degree that we feel separation, we experience pain.

Life is not about proving who you are, life is about being who you are. Seek your purpose for being, and live with passion. When you feel passion, you'll know you're following your purpose.

You are bound only by your tethers of fear...
Each new step of faith cuts an old cord. When you're ready to fly, you will release what you thought was keeping you safe and let your imagination free.

One of the greatest gifts that parents can give to a child, is Showing them the beauty of a loving relationship.

It's an ignorant man that doesn't seek out his own faults.

You can only feel something when there is some resistance. This resistance is vibrated through shock waves in all directions. The resistance is what causes reaction. Action and reaction are building blocks of creation.

The shell of a man is fragile, the ego is the barrier to his true self.

Belief in the familiar is often

An escape of accountability.

A single step of faith brings both death and a renewed life.
The fearful part of yourself is now released with great
appreciation for having served its purpose in our life.
Then, with each new step in awareness, we shed an old belief.
Be bold and let go...

FEAR

The vigorous defense of one's belief and the willingness to kill over one's belief is insanity and completely rooted in fear. More specifically, any passage within any teaching that is rooted in fear is either misunderstood or intentionally written to create fear. Fear is man's only true obstacle.

When a heart imagines that it can be broken,
it withdraws from sharing what should have been spoken.
Remember that love not shared is missed...
But not lost... so give the love that you are, whatever the cost.

The answers to your questions are not found in words.
They are found in your feelings; learn to trust them.

Until you've seen something from multiple perspectives,
You haven't really seen it at all.

It is both a choice and a gift to receive wisdom from
another man's experience. Most often, another man's
experience is merely recited as an event. Rarely is the event of
another owned as if you were there.

PERCEPTION

Our perception of life has everything to do with what we believe. We should be continually seeking new perspectives to have any real grasp of reality. Even though Reality is relative, we must always be seeking a greater understanding of everything, or settle for a very limited life experience. Just imagine what we don't know. Look at what we have discovered within the last 100 years, basically one human lifetime… cars, telephones, television, radios and computers. The gravity of what we've accomplished is staggering, yet the growing awareness of what we don't know is even more impressive.

This earth is about 4.5 billion years old, and man has been on this earth for a tiny percentage of that time. There is so much to learn once we just realize that we are here to experience life through our exploration of self. To be wrong, should be a grand revelation because it means that we were going in the wrong direction. Re-calibration is a good thing if you're genuinely looking for the truth. To explore means to reach outside of ourselves and find our truth, to remove the boundaries of fear and superstition. As many great Masters have tried to explain; seek first, and you will find the kingdom. This is what life's all about. Seek, don't settle.

THE PROCESS OF SPIRITUALITY

Believe it or not, spirituality seems to be a learned trait. Even though we are born as spiritual beings, we are also apparently born unaware of everything. All of our senses are completely new and overwhelming. Light is painful and piercing, sounds are penetrating, and even touch can be awkward and invasive.

At the beginning of life, everything is new. It's only through the moment-by-moment process of discovering the meaning of each new bit of information that life begins to make sense. Out of the light eventually comes form, out of the sounds comes communication, and out of touch emerges the tapestry of discovery.

Each discovery is a building block that allows a new level of understanding for every new discovery. Most new discoveries, or new levels of awareness, are made possible by projecting new thoughts onto old ideas. This means that you couldn't have come to the conclusion you did, without the benefit of the old information. This how we learn, and once we understand that life is a process, we can then better prepare ourselves, and others, for the winding road of self-discovery and enlightenment.

The process of enlightenment is just that, a process. Although it may seem that one day... Wow! The light comes on. It all makes sense. The reality is that it's the beginning of your conscious awareness through newly opened eyes. It may also have simultaneously allowed for the reconciliation of past events that now, seem to make perfect sense. This is a very mechanical definition of the process of awakening. However, the attainment of awareness is anything but mechanical. It's a beautiful journey that culminates in a burst of emotion; a realization of oneness and wholeness that embodies your spirit.

The brain is our primary tool for operating in this dimension. It's not only our computer; it acts as an operating system as well. The cool thing about both our computer and its mode of operation are that neither is static. This means that both components physically change to meet our new demands. The brain seems to be hard-wired to perform specific tasks.

Beliefs are often responsible for the lack of responsibility on one's part. You've probably heard someone say, "I'm just wired that way." Well for that moment it's true, they *are* wired that way.

Not everyone is aware of this, but the brain is capable of re-wiring itself... literally. As new ideas and information are introduced, the brain tries to find ways to process this new data. When the new data appears more and more frequently, the brain begins to build new pathways to process the new information. Eventually, the new pathways are strong enough to become the dominant route for this new information. At this point, the old pathway starts to break away, and the new path... is the new you.

Fortunately, and sometimes unfortunately, this process works for just about everything. This is how addictions are created as well. As a substance is consistently introduced to the body, the brain reacts with a chemical response. These chemicals are called peptides. These are strong pheromone type chemicals that evoke a specific physical response. Depending on the type and amount of the substance that is introduced, the brain will decide how to handle this new sensation. With some drugs, the new receptors and pathways will develop extremely quickly, thus creating an almost instant addiction in some individuals.

For those of us that are seeking greater awareness in our lives, we can take great pleasure in understanding that our life is not a hard-wired destiny. Our life is our creation, and we create through an expanded awareness; this how our body/mind works. Our brain is an amazing tool that works to provide what we ask. The key to creating is consistency. Ever wonder why the more you do something, the easier it gets. That's your brain adapting. Amazing isn't it!!!

The spiritual path works much the same way, but instead of just a physical process, you have the non-physical or metaphysical processes as well. The term metaphysical, can imply universal energy. When one can understand that everything in the universe is made of the same infinite waves and particles of energy, including ourselves, then we can begin to consciously create from a whole new perspective. We create from energy, as energy. This is where creation takes a quantum leap. As you become conscious, you come alive.

*A*n Angel is love, manifest as hope.

*K*arma and opportunity are two sides of the same coin.

*M*editation in its highest form is listening,
you can't receive if you don't listen.

A conscious life is not about concepts; it's about experiences.
This is why the truth cannot be explained or proselytized.
It must be discovered.

*R*egarding religion or any spiritual teachings...
Hopefully with time, you will forget the words
and just live their intention.

CRAZY MOJO

Whether you're standing in line at the store, at your office, or anywhere else, your inner vibrational state of being is continuously sending out energy that is directly reflected in your surroundings. Your day-to-day experiences will be a good snapshot of your general state of being. This is especially apparent when you're driving. Most of what we do while driving is very unconscious, and thus is a great indicator of our current state of being. If your life seems a little wild and crazy, you may have to look deep in the mirror to see why.

All of our thoughts and especially our feelings are continuously sending out strong vibrations in the form of energy waves. When people say things like, "I don't know why this keeps happening to me," it's most likely because the energy they're sending out, crazy mojo, feels like irritating static to everyone around them. The people around you will be responding to your irritating vibrational frequency. They'll feel frustrated for no apparent reason. This is cause and effect on an energetic level.

Some people enjoy driving, and others experience driving as a battle of survival. The way you experience life is a direct reflection of your inner state of being. I promise you, if someone is especially rude to you, whether you're driving or standing still, you're sending out some crazy mojo. Your energy is *that* powerful. You may feel like you're minding your own business... not a chance!!!

Curiosity is the light... shed unto darkness.

When the infinite eyes of wisdom are clouded by faith,
the truth will surely fade into darkness.

Where wisdom stands on clarity,
knowledge leans on belief.

Science is only as good as what we understand about the
results. The interpretation of the observation is the variable.

Our finite perceptions about what we see are clouded by our limited view of reality. What we know is finite, what we don't know is infinite. Therefore, much of science is theory, especially in the quantum realm. Since we know that all energy and matter are connected, it makes sense how the mere observation of some experiments changes the outcome. Energy has its unique intelligence and is quite capable of interacting with us through our inherent connection. Science is still interpreting results as a mechanistic process; they are calculating assessments of a perceived outcomes. As yet there is little spiritual curiosity within science. These two worlds will eventually collide in a universal acknowledgment of our unified reality. Everything exists within multiple dimensions, including consciousness. This is the missing link for scientists.

The perception that we are many creates the illusion that we are separate from each other. We are manifest as children, but all of one divine mother.

Thoughts are like radio signals. The more powerful the focus behind the thought, the farther the reach and ability to create. Thought energy is always sent and received. It always creates. If you're not happy with your creations, you might want to reconcile what you think about most.

Love and compassion are the keys to creation. With love being the stable foundation, and compassion being original thought, then creation is the natural reaction as we evolve. Life seeks to sustain life. The nature of nature is to nurture, to bring forth life. The cause is compassion, and the effect is creation through movement.

A strong leader knows, tact and reason,
will outlive his stubborn force of will.
Balance your life:
Give equal attention and favor,
For the fruits of your labor will be
spoiled and not savored.

When you believe in light, you only see with your eyes.
When you believe in words, you only hear what you want.
When you feel with your soul, you can believe in yourself.

Trust begets freedom.

The perfect balance of push and pull, yin and yang, are what forms the ocean waves and creates our world. As the water is pushed from the top and pulled from the bottom, the waves break and stir the womb of creation. Our ocean is the mighty mother that through her tireless motion gives life.

"Just because" is the reason that nobody knows; it's the reason with virtue, that is never deposed.

Activities don't create our experiences; our personal experiences are created through our emotional interpretation of the physical event.

No man has fear until his imagination outgrows his sense of reality.

MASTERING YOUR BREATH

Mastering your breath is the key to mastering your Life. Your first breath in begins this life, and your last breath out will end it. Between your first and last breath lie the fuel and the key for living. When we learn to control the volume and intensity of our breath, we can begin to understand the immense power that we have within ourselves. Our breath fuels the spark that unleashes everything. It gives our body's unlimited strength, our soul's unfettered movement, and it's the first step in quieting the mind. We can traverse the universe through our will and our breath. As we discover the power of breathing, we discover the power of living without limits. You will discover that by finding your breath, you will find your life. Breathing air is an impulse that only sustains life; a conscious breath will create a conscious moment.

THE REAL YOU

We are one in spirit, unique in mind, with a purpose of expression and remembrance. We are the eyes, ears, and the touch of God, as we create our experiences. As we remember our truly divine nature, we can experience hardships as our greatest gifts. We see not only the silver linings but also the golden heart, that heals through our growth. When we begin to see life through compassionate eyes, we begin to live. The real you is everywhere, and in everything. The real you exists as eternal love, expressing itself as life.

FREQUENCIES

The things that we see are only frequencies of light that are interpreted as objects. We see solid objects as matter because we cannot see how fast the light/energy is moving. It's moving so fast it appears to be still. It's only a matter of perception. Our collective consciousness agrees that certain frequencies equal certain physicalities. This is only a three-dimensional agreement. The other dimensions are not bound by this agreement. This is why the body is not needed outside of this dimension. Thought energy is boundless. Reality is relative to one's understanding of the creative process.

Enriched soil not only provides the environment for growth, it attracts that which is most likely to thrive. Our relationships work from the same law of attraction. When we enrich our own soil, we attract that which is most likely to thrive as well. True relationships start from the inside, not from searching outside. Just look at nature... when the soil is ready, beautiful creations emerge.

Cause for thought is a good thing.
Thought just because, is a bad habit.

Don't resist right now... just flow.

You've been riding the brakes; it's time to let go.
Momentum will guide you as you roll with the waves,
So loosen your grip, it's time to be BRAVE!

Only an empty vessel, can be filled.

Only a quiet mind, can hear the truth.
Only an open heart, can feel compassion.
Only a clear conscience, can live in the moment.

SOCIAL DYSFUNCTION

I'm certainly not a doctor of any kind, but I do have a perspective of spiritual psychology, which allows me to see things from a broader perspective, than most traditional forms of psychology. From my perspective, I've experienced that many "social disorders" as they're commonly referred to, are caused by living within and around chaotic environments for extended periods of time. I've also observed that many of the people in these environments wouldn't call their environment chaotic. They don't see the dysfunction. They just experience the victimization and depression related to not being in control. The traditional belief is that people with social disorders have an illness, and their illness causes them to make chaotic, dysfunctional decisions.

In some instances, I'm sure this is true. There could be a legitimate physical cause, but I believe that in a great many cases, we have allowed one's unconscious mind to be programmed by the chaotic external stimulus, resulting in chaotic, repetitive, unconscious behavior.

Once this perspective is understood, I would think that this point of view could create a sense of empowerment. You would no longer see yourself as the victim of an illness. You do, however, have to take responsibility for your thoughts. Once you learn to take control of your thoughts, you can take control of your life.

As you read on, I offer suggestions on how to regain control of your conscious mind. The unconscious mind, as the "ruler" of your actions, is in charge, until the conscious mind, actually thinks about what it's doing.

Unconscious living is one's reaction to an environment instead of creating it. Most people are subconsciously reacting to life in one way or another, therefore, are subject to all of the influences around them.

I've known some very normal people that after spending enough time in a chaotic or neurotic environment have picked up chaotic traits to a substantial degree. In my opinion, most personal social disorder seems to be the epitome of unconscious behavior. Today's child rearing is a perfect example. Giving the social disorder a title removes the personal responsibility, and provides a layer of insulation from criticism.

Becoming self-accountable is the first step in true recovery, even for children. This applies to any other addiction or social disorder as well. Learning conscious awareness is the first step in recovering your life.

You can begin with some basic meditation techniques for a start. There are many resources for different types of meditation that you can get comfortable with.

Calming your mind is the first step in controlling your life. I once heard someone say, "I had to stop meditating because my thoughts kept getting in the way." This is what I'm talking about.

The mind is not your Master. It's like the old saying, "who's in charge here?" If you're not in control of your mind, then who is?

Learning to be the observer of your life is another way to gain control. You must be able to step outside of yourself to better see your whole self from a broader perspective. It's sort of like watching yourself on TV.

Remember the first time that you heard a recording of your own voice? Or saw yourself on a TV monitor? It seems odd at first. Most people don't see themselves as other people do. We're looking outside, while they're looking in.

There's a much bigger difference than that, though. Most people are totally unaware of their unconscious behavior. For all practical purposes, this means that they don't see in themselves what everyone else sees in them. They're always pointing the finger of blame in the other direction.

Unconscious living creates personal and social chaos. It's not a disorder; it's a disassociation of any conscious behavior. If one can muster up enough self-control to ask one's self, "Why am I doing this?" then you have a chance to see who you really are. This gives you a chance to be your own judge, event by event. You gain self-control and self-awareness; one conscious thought at a time; one conscious breath at a time. Remember reacting to life is not living, it's just surviving.

The conscious mind as powerful as it is is still creating from a state of separateness. When the conscious mind realizes that it is actually the mind of consciousness with a unique perspective, it will fly with no limits.

Fear is the darkness that hides the truth. When the light of infinite love illuminates your path, the road to your true self will be clear to see.

What we consider to be miracles are just awakenings into reality.

Our ego and pride, sit by our side, Posing to serve us, yet clearly enslave us.

Give thanks to the brave hearts of men, certain of self and deed…. they are men of bold character, willing to dare, and to bleed.

To name something, is not to know something this is true, but to name something with joy in your heart… this is good too.

If life were a video game, how would you play it? Would you be the hero or the villain? Would it be an action movie or a love story? Think about what you would create, and why you're not.

Confidence comes from inner strength; arrogance comes from inner fear.

Life's natural course is not to pull or persuade; it's to honor this moment for its purpose and its grace.

The primary difference between judgment and observation is the level of emotion attached to the event.

Messages through time, written in parables and rhymes, were constructed in truth, but their meaning now blind.

When doors seem to open easily and the path seems clear, it's because your will and intention are in harmony with this point in time. Your will is what creates motion, divine harmony is what brings it into existence.

How can you be free if you're afraid of the unknown?

Trust and dishonesty are two sides of the same coin.
Make sure you're in charge of it.

The actions of most are fearful and feeble, followers by nature, more like sheep than people. To be bold and unique is rare indeed... for what rules men's hearts are worries and needs. To play safe is to settle for what you've been told, so live each day to discover and unfold

Life is a journey of treasures, I'm told, it's about self-discovery, and not about gold. A mission can make a man that needs a good test, but the man on a mission will lead all the rest. It's not the mission that determines the strength of a man. It's how a man discovers himself when he stops to listen.

To science is knowledge, as spirit is to wisdom,
each is a path to truth.

TO BE HAPPY…

To be happy and feel loved; this seems to be at the top of most people's list. I'm sure these seem like basic needs to some, and a completely unobtainable dream to others. The problem in either circumstance is that this model places love and happiness *outside* of one's self. Love and happiness cannot be bestowed upon us; they are feelings that we discover within ourselves as we become self-aware. Love and happiness are inherent qualities that we each embody. The illusion is that we must get love and happiness; the reality is that we are love and happiness. The illusion of separateness is the source of our confusion.

I am but a single ray of light, emanating from an infinite source. I am a single perspective among an infinite collective. I am an experience within the boundaries of my belief. I exist as an expression of life as what I create. I am the gift of life as an expression of love; we are one.

The soul is part of a collective experience with a unique perspective. This unique experience expands the whole of collective consciousness. This allows the collective consciousness to physically experience life. A conceptual experience is only a story; it's only imagined. When Imagination is brought to life, it's called creation.

ACCOUNTABILITY

What are some of the limiting factors involved in keeping you from fulfilling your potential? Our body and our mind are capable of incredible transformations simply by altering what we eat, how we exercise, or don't exercise, and most importantly how we think and feel about ourselves. This is why we have to come to grip with being accountable for where we are now. This accountability bestows great power on the dedicated. You have to be brutally honest with yourself first. Power comes from surrender, and then from within one's self, arises the ability to see the truth.

The Buddha stated it this way. "There is no knowledge won without sacrifice. In order to gain anything, you must first lose everything." This statement describes how one must first release the attachments of our egotistical mind. Release the illusion that worldly possessions that define our value. The balance of our mind, in the acceptance of our transient nature of life, is one of the keys to internal peace.

We are not required to give up material things, but one must simply see that these material things aid in our lives, they do not define the value of our lives. This realization allows for an ebb and flow of relationships and material possessions without the pain or fear of loss. As we begin to honor each life or object that crosses our path, we can share in the gratitude that all of life's experiences are precious moments to embrace.

Each experience serves a higher purpose in everyone's life. Part of our purpose is to grow through each experience.

I found a comfortable place inside of myself that feels like the truth.

What appears to be chaos is merely the coming together of polarities.

When we learn to understand that change is the driving force of creation, we can then be at peace with what is and not remorse in our loss. Peace brings with it a greater understanding of the creative process. When we're at peace, we create naturally by attracting that which is in harmony with our chosen purpose. A good measure of your spiritual nature is how well you and "change" get along.

LEAD BY EXAMPLE

Life is meant to be experienced in incremental levels. One could use the term, level of consciousness, or states of awareness. The purpose of each level is to acquire vital lessons essential for building a stable personal foundation. When we're given, or exposed to things that are beyond our current understanding by any term, we're incapable of dealing with it in any responsible way. One example is what often happens to professional athletes. They are often thrust into a spotlight far beyond their current ability to cope with fame and fortune. Many of them will stumble and find themselves in trouble or even financially devastated. The athletes that pursue guidance and are willing to learn can avoid many pitfalls; they will have built a strong foundation to build upwards.

Another example is children that are exposed to extreme violence through movies, video games, or even neighborhood bullies or gangs. It doesn't matter what form it comes it. It's not possible for these kids to rationalize what they're experiencing. Whatever they see becomes part of their operating program and straight into their subconscious mind. Their minds are being re-wired to a new normal, and their thoughts become a reflection of this violent inner experience. We're seeing more and more kids living out these violent new fantasies. To them, it is perfectly "normal." It's a manifestation of this newly programmed consciousness. It is so important that we let our children be children, and learn responsibility through guidance and experience, step by step.

We, as a "civilized culture," have failed. We have not become civilized, we, as a culture have become demoralized. Not by religious standards, but by human standards. We have become a product of our runaway unconscious behavior, and have allowed the addiction of needing more and more to rule our lives. We need more stuff, we need more time, we need more excitement, and we need to be entertained. This *need* for more and more stimulus has created this extreme environment. It's like any addiction; you need more and more of a thing to maintain the effect. The only way to save ourselves is to wake up. Everything in life is co-created. That means that as "adults" we are supposed to be more consciously aware than our children. If they have gone off-track, then it's our responsibility to guide them back. The days of lazy parenting should come to an end. Excuses must be transformed into accountability. Until we are capable of accepting responsibility for what we have created, we are incapable of consciously creating change. Followers make excuses, and leaders make other leaders. *Lead* your children or they will lead you into chaos. Just look around. How many parents are parenting vs. how many are making excuses? A parent should be a leader. If you can't lead your children, then get out of the way and let the teachers have the power to actually teach again. Schools are a place to learn about life. Life is about respect, responsibility, and compassion. These are things that we learn through guidance.

If you love your children, then lead them, if you don't know, how then seek answers. The only way you can fail is not to try. With action comes answers, and with this new vision comes hope. Learn to be the change your children need to see and learn to see in your children all that they can be.

Excuses beget followers, and accountability begets leaders.

Messages often come as a whisper, so listen carefully. This is why I say that unless you have something important to share, share the silence.

The experience is the purpose, so don't let your expectations cloud the truth. The truth is not what you see; It's what you become.

To accept for the truth a story that's told,

is to accept in yourself a fate yet untold. To seek your own truth, with a diligent mind, brings forth new passions and blessings to find.

PINGS AND VIBRATIONS

To resist something, you have to actually either physically or emotionally hold on to it in some way. The idea that you must let go of something to get rid of it is just common sense. Life becomes so much easier when we learn to release issues before they become problems or drama in our life. Release, is a literal requirement, not just a suggestion. If there is still something in your life that is an issue or bothering you, then you haven't completely let it go of it. It's not possible for something to still be in your life if you've completely let it go. If you're still feeling the pain or anxiety of something, it's because there is still at least one thread of attachment. Even the tiniest thread of residual connection is enough to trigger a response. Nature always has good examples of everything. Look at how a spider web works. The tiniest filaments are strung out as far as the spider can reach to catch his next meal. The spider can feel the tiniest vibration in the web because he's connected to it.

Our lives operate much the same way. Everywhere we go, and even every time we think of someone, we create a filament of energy. Every time we think, or move in that direction, we create a vibration that is felt on the other end of that filament. This happens everywhere, all the time, and we're usually oblivious to it and wonder why certain issues never go away. This is because as tiny as the connection is, it's still a connection. Another good example is sonar. Whether it's a

Bat or a Submarine, the sonar signals are looking for something to bounce off of, and when they do it's called a Ping.

Each time you focus on someone even in the slightest way, you're sending out a signal, and they get *pinged*. The more power there is behind thought, the stronger the *ping*. Their subconscious feels the *ping* and then reacts in some way. How many times have you just thought of someone and then within minutes or seconds that person called or came by? One of you pinged the other. The same thing happens via our emotions. Our vibrations are always felt on the other end, maybe not consciously, but certainly subconsciously. This is how it works.

Everything in our life is co-created on some level because we are all connected to each other and everything, all the time. Be aware of what vibration you're sending out. You might not like what you get back.

"Good Vibrations" work the same way. Focus intently and watch amazing things happen around you.

THE FRAGILE FAÇADE

The emotional state that one may gravitate to in a tough situation is most likely their true nature. Many people have a very fragile facade that falls away when they lose conscious attention of their emotions. It's this conscious attention that reminds the subconscious mind to stay in control.

When one's conscious attention is diverted, the subconscious habits take over. This is a good reason to spend plenty time with someone before committing to a long-term relationship. People become very adept at putting up a false front to avoid embarrassment by their true nature. A great way to gauge one's true nature is by watching them drive a car. A lot of people can "talk the talk," but take a little drive with them and see what shows up.

To live an honest life, you have to feel whom you are inside. This self-awareness is where inner peace resides.

Within the gift of awareness, is peace.

I Can

To me, the idea that you have to *identify* with an addiction, to cure it, is very counterproductive. It's the subjugated identification of the issue that keeps the condition a part of your life. Identifying with something allows the mind to create a place for the situation to hang out. Once you identify with something, you've created a bond, a type of emotional relationship that makes it nearly impossible to get rid of.

Why would someone name something, make a place for it, think and talk about it often, then ask it to leave? To release something, you have actually to let it go. It's acknowledging that the condition is not a part of you that releases it. In my opinion, many traditional approaches to treatment only provide a means of coping. These organizations have great intentions, but I would say that many of their members still consider themselves victims in some way.

When you identify with something, you bring it to life. As soon as you say the words, hi my name is... and I'm a... you just created and gave birth to a new self-created entity. It's now your story; your cross to bear. This is not healing; it's coping. Healing is about releasing restrictions in our body and our minds. It's about identifying with the concept of wholeness and understanding that we are not a finite concept of self-identity.

We're here to awaken to our true nature as creators and to

experience ourselves through the process of making conscious choices. This means not only choosing what to do but more importantly, how to think and how to productively use our emotions. Using our emotions as the fuel to create momentum is how we create our experiences. Our enthusiasm is literally what makes us move. Think about it.

What do you do if you're depressed? Usually sleep, eat, or complain about something. There's no movement or call to action for anything. The first part of enthusiasm is the initial concept, the *'I can'* moment. Then as you visualize the concept, your mind begins to create options.

Once you make your first choice, you've set something into motion. Motion doesn't have to be just physical motion. Each intentional thought creates waves of energy that create from different planes. When you combine intense thought and intense action, you are moving mountains. The point here is to move forward by acknowledging your inner wisdom and accepting your ability to choose your life.

Branding yourself with a scarlet letter serves no high purpose. Acknowledge the experience, be grateful for it, and then release the pain and claim the greatness in your higher purpose. Through meditation, study, and a desire to move forward, you will find the means to accomplish anything you apply your focus to. Don't stop to identify with the past in any way. Be grateful for all experiences, then live in the now.

YOU CAN!

Compassion

Compassion can only come from a reasonable understanding or awareness of something. In general, the greater your level of awareness, the greater your level of compassion. When I talk about compassion, I'm talking about the heartfelt emotion that drives your thoughts and ultimately your action regarding the subject. A great example is an activist versus the pacifist.

An activist will usually have a deeper understanding and awareness of a subject than the average person. The pacifist may just be less aware of the depth of an issue and not see the urgency or significance of the issue. The lack of compassion about anything doesn't show an intentional disdain for something; it shows that they don't fully understand the issue. This is true whether it's a negotiation or a physical circumstance. People will kill each other because they can't see anything, but their personal point of view. This lack of awareness may also reveal the lack of desire to see the truth.

THE HIGHER PERSPECTIVE

An analogy for expanding your level of consciousness is sort of like climbing a ladder. Each new level gives us a new perspective or a new level of awareness. As we strive for new or higher levels, we can now see more and more from this new perspective. The higher we get, the broader our perspective. What happens though, is that most people get afraid of heights, so to speak. These higher levels bring uncertainty so many people will stop climbing, and stay at a more comfortable level. This is true physically and metaphysically. Everyone has their personal sense of how far they would like to go, and what will usually hold them back, is fear. Climbing to higher awareness is no different than climbing a tall ladder or climbing a mountain. You have to feel capable of going higher before you will.

When you're comfortable at a level and consider that level stable, then it's psychologically easier to take the next step. Spiritually speaking, this new awareness can shake up your sense of stability; that's the scariest thing of all. When people's sense of self-identity is shaken, they usually back off and move to more comfortable territory. If you're genuinely seeking the truth, you have to consider that your old reality was just an old belief; you have to be willing to look a little deeper. Belief, for the sake of belief, doesn't carry much value. To seek the truth, you have to see words as information and gather as much information as you can from as many perspectives as possible. If you're only looking through one source or limited sources, then you're very likely just looking for comfort in your current belief. We grow by stretching our boundaries, and through the willingness to leave behind information that doesn't serve us anymore.

The first people to announce that the earth wasn't flat, or that the earth isn't the center of the universe, I'm sure, shook up a lot of belief systems. Those beliefs were integral to who or what we thought we were. Ultimately those beliefs had to be shed to evolve towards a broader view of our evolving reality. Our sense of reality will always evolve, as our understanding of life evolves. When we stop seeking the truth, we'll only see what we believe. Our purpose is to evolve, and you shouldn't settle for being less than all that you can imagine. Only your fear has held you back, now let your curiosity create your future.

For those of you whose sky is always falling, it's the fear in your heart, and not your true calling. When we experience this world as a fearful place, we draw ever closer this fear we embrace. So as we attract what we fear, and experience the pain... we may feel the sky falling, but it's only the rain.

THE GENUINE JOURNEY

There is a conceptual and experiential element to almost everything. You will always lack true understanding of a subject without the experience of it... and even when you do have an experience, you need to have a high level of awareness about the experience for it to have a significant impact.

Teaching, or even repeating something from a conceptual position can open up a real can of worms if something is not interpreted accurately, or a vital perspective is missed. Even having the experience still only gives you *your* perspective of that experience. You can see how limited you would be if you're only reading or hearing about something. As the saying goes, "*until you've walked a mile in another man's shoes,* you can't' experience where he's been."

OUR PURPOSE

Part of our objective in this life experience is to discover what our purpose is and then, begin to live from that new awareness. Fortunately, our higher purpose is embedded within our daily experiences, even without our conscious awareness of it. Imagine what we can create for both ourselves and for those around us with this elevated conscious understanding of who we really are.

Our lives are formed by our beliefs, and our beliefs are only thoughts. When we shift our thoughts towards the quest of higher understanding, we can move mountains. This higher understanding allows us to move through obstacles, instead of being held back. You have within your being, the power of your source; it can be no other way. When you allow the student within you to seek the "Truth" behind any teaching, you will experience your *true* potential in this life experience. You'll no longer be an island; you'll see that your horizon has no boundaries. Truth is the ultimate reality that lies within consciousness, and you are part of this consciousness to the degree that you accept and evolve within consciousness. Life is your choice. Become the student, and see who you really are.

The soul is part of a collective experience with a unique perspective. This unique experience expands the whole of collective consciousness. This allows the collective consciousness to physically experience life. A conceptual experience is only a story; it's only imagined. When Imagination is brought to life, it's called creation.

Teach, and you will discover a passion you can't hide. The passion is not the teaching, but the discovery inside.

OUR SPIRITUAL BEGINNINGS

In our spiritual beginnings, we are mostly speaking *about* subjects, and not *from* the experience. Until we have actually experienced something, we're limited in our understanding. Take swimming for example. You can't read a book and know for certain what swimming will be like. You won't know until you're *in* the water what you're going to experience. The actual experience will be different for everyone. Some will sink, some will float, some will panic, and some will experience pure joy.

Experiencing spirituality is very much the same scenario. Once you've experienced a dimension beyond what we can see, you'll see everything in life very differently. You can't un-know an experience. Once you've experienced this broader perspective, you will have seen the broader implications of the big picture. By default, the more experiences you pull together, the better idea you have of what your purpose is, relative to the bigger picture. You don't have to have all the answers, or collect all the answers to have an understanding of what you're dealing with. You do, however, have to start seeking the truth. If you're relying on what other people are telling you about life, you will have to settle for their understanding of what they see. This is how most people gather their information, second or third hand, with a little judgment mixed in. The image that one pulls together in this way is not really a picture of anything. It's a collection of illusions that feed a common belief that keeps everyone working on the same picture. It keeps them busy, and most importantly, it gives them a purpose; it makes them a team player. Before we achieve some initial level of awareness, very little of our behavior is conscious. Very few people will live consciously enough to find their own way in this universe.

Awareness requires a great deal of attention and time, to begin to see the patterns that will emerge through your effort. Life becomes an endless accumulation of events that form your experiences. Each validated piece of experience will eventually find its place, and when you finally put enough of them together, you'll have that big "Ah-Ha" moment. A lot of people mistake this for the moment of enlightenment. This is just the beginning of learning how to live consciously. Conscious living is the gift that most will leave unopened. Claim your gift and begin to experience why you're here. The choice is yours, and the life that you experience is yours to create.

As you seek the truth within each experience, remember that within this multidimensional framework, many of your accumulated experiences will exist within each other. It may take many separate experiences to make sense of one concept. The better that you understand the concept, the broader your perspective becomes.

You'll eventually become very comfortable working within this multi-dimensional reality. You'll soon actually experience how it works. This understanding will not only grow with each passing day; it will grow with each new incarnation. There are many dimensions to everything.

As a student, we should always be seeking a greater understanding of ourselves. Ironically though, part of the greater understanding is, to live in gratitude for each moment... *just as it is.*

A TRIP TO THE BOTTOM

Living in fear is like living in quicksand. Ever wonder why you often sink deeper and deeper. When you continually struggle through life, damning the world for all your problems, you're actually working yourself closer to the bottom. Struggle, whether it's physically or mentally, will ultimately take you down.

Instead, sit still with your body and your mind... and in *this* moment... be grateful. Feel gratitude with every cell in your body. This intense gratitude is what heals everything within and around you. Now... with a clear view... you can begin to see the miracles around you and how many new paths there are to choose from. Life is about listening within, and when you do, you'll never be without. Listening is the beginning of silence. Silence is where the answers reside.

SYNONYMOUS

Creation and evolution are synonymous, as are causation and unfoldment, energy, Matter and intelligence: in all cases, they represent multiple perspectives of one reality. They're integrally a part of each other and objectively pointing in the same direction. There is no opposition at all except within a narrow, biased interpretation; that *bias* can be from any one perspective. Once your heart is open to the deepest purpose of these words, you'll see that they have the same Divine essence.

The reason that I mention that these words are synonymous is because some spiritual teachers and even scientists draw a sort of *'hard line'* in describing one of these words over the other.

One example would be the description of life as the unfolding of Divine potential, versus the Causation of life. In causation, one could say, that we are what we are because we evolved as a result of something. The unfolding of divine potential, to me, is the awakening of energy into life. They are just different ways of saying, "I am, that I am." Or maybe, I am what I am. An acorn will ultimately be an oak tree. A tadpole will be a frog, and you and I started as single cells. We are all evolving through consciousness in order to experience our true nature. None of this would not be possible without the inherent collective force within our universe.

The cause of two entities equals the creation of more. You can't have creation without an underlying driving force, and you can't have cause without creation. Without a push and pull, there would be no movement. Without yin, there could be no yang. Balance is the basis for creation.

Within each resides, a demon we hide, it's a piece of the past we no longer confide. This demon has wings and can fly on a whim, it's part of our being not a her or a him. This part of our past, now a tool for our soul, gives us clear vision, our new conscious goal.

BEING AN EMPTY VESSEL

The Tao Te Ching teaches us that emptiness is the key to living. So you're probably thinking, that doesn't sound like any fun. Well, if you're looking at the emptiness as an empty life, then you'd probably be right. Fortunately, that's not what it means. When the Tao talks about emptiness being the key to living, it's referring to being open, receptive, and connected, but un-attached. There's an old saying: "It's hard to fill a cup that is already full." This means that until we accept that we don't have all the answers, we're not likely to be open to new ideas. This goes much deeper than just being receptive to new ideas. To hear any guidance from our spiritual partners, we must have a clear connection that is only possible through a calm spirit. This can happen through many forms of meditation.

We have to open our hearts, clear our minds, accept the past, and live in this moment. Tomorrow is only a projection that may or may not come. If we're not creating from within, then we're allowing what is outside of ourselves to create who we are. As we develop ourselves, we create our environment. This is the difference between creating vs. reacting. By embracing each moment as a gift, we can live each moment as an opportunity. This is how we begin to open our hearts. This is how the cycle of creation starts and how we can begin to share our life through each experience. As we share, we open the hearts of others, and the world begins to come alive. When we live as *one* through the consciousness of the whole, we begin to realize our true state of being.

Through living a conscious life, we create space. As we gradually remove the clutter that fills up space around us, and within us, we can begin to see, feel, and hear the truth. It's by creating this emptiness, (an open vessel,) which we create the space to live.

SEEING YOUR ROLE IN LIFE

It's not enough to say that you want to be something or to accomplish a specific goal. To truly live consciously, one must not only discover, or live some purpose, but one must consciously live that purpose for the betterment of the whole. This means that you have to see your role, and know that you are consciously playing a part in the evolution of life itself. Living consciously means that you understand how each thought and action creates our environment. The more conscious choices we make, the more aware the world becomes.

CONTEMPLATION

The difference between thought and contemplation is the power behind it. Random thoughts are sort of like a rowboat crossing a pond. It makes ripples in the pond but doesn't change anything. Contemplation, on the other hand, has much more energy behind it. It's more like a ski boat throwing out wakes that rearrange the shorelines; there's a much greater impact on the pond as a whole. Remember that everything is energy, and all energy moves. When we contemplate deeply, we make things move. Contemplative action, followed by physical action, is how we create great things.

LETTING GO

Learning to let go of something needs to become as automatic as waving off a fly. Think about how things come up in your head. Thoughts show up and distract our attention from what we should be doing, or thinking about. Instead of allowing these distractions to completely throw us off track, we need to learn to shake them off; one swipe and let it go. If it comes back, swipe it away again... let it go. Thoughts, just like the flies, can often be persistent, but they will go away if we don't dwell on the problem. The reality here is that you do have complete control over your thoughts. The flies, not so much! As you get better at shaking off random thoughts, you'll begin to re-gain control of your life. You'll start to become more conscious, self-aware, and confident. The first step in conscious living is learning to let go.

YOUR EGO

Your view of the past significantly impacts your future. When you see the past as a series of traumas or mistakes, you have confirmed to your subconscious mind that you are not in control of anything; consequently, your subconscious mind will continue to rule your abandoned conscious mind.

Without attention, your subconscious mind is dominant. It requires diligent effort and training to teach your *conscious mind* how to step up and be the leader in your life.

One of the hardest parts of this growth process is accepting personal responsibility for your life, as it is now. Your subconscious mind likes to play the victim and blame life on everyone else. This is how it relinquishes responsibility. It sounds odd that your subconscious mind can rule your conscious mind, but what happens is, your conscious mind has been programmed by your subconscious mind to take a back seat.

Often one's conscious mind is barely even aware of itself. Your ego will always step up to run your life because your ego lives *its life* through you. Your ego-centered self-identity has its own agenda and is a powerful force in your life. Your ego will convince you that your life *is just what it is*, and you're not the problem, everyone else is.

The ego is what you could call your evil twin. It's not evil, but the decisions that your ego will make on its own, will most likely not move you towards any notably high purpose. It may keep you safe in some ways, but it will always hold you back from any self-realization.

Conscious thinking, and the actual creation of your future requires movement. It means you have to stop standing in your old footsteps and start making new ones. Every new footstep is a step of conscious creation. Your subconscious will consider this risk... your conscious mind can take the opportunity to grow.

Our actions are representative of our thoughts, and our thoughts are our tools that we create with. As long as your thoughts are that of the victim, you'll have to relinquish any control over your life. Since victims only react to life circumstances, they're at the whim of whom, and whatever is going on around them.

You have to accept responsibility for your life to have any sense of control. Accepting responsibility means making conscious decisions based on your life's purpose and goals. If you're not making conscious decisions, then your subconscious mind is making them. The subconscious mind is the program for the unconscious mind. Your subconscious mind is full of stuff that your friends, family, churches, government, and the media want you to think or believe.

We're constantly bombarded with information that in one way or another sinks into our subconscious mind. It's important to form your own beliefs, and question anyone or any organization that uses any form of fear, to sway your thoughts or actions. Fear is a great motivator, but not for the empowered human with a conscious mind.

When your conscious mind is engaged, you are creating your world. As long as your subconscious mind is driving your decisions, your life is just a series of reactions and someone else's agenda. When you engage your conscious mind, you will begin to see that the world is not the bottomless pit of sorrow and pain that all victims share. It's a world of purpose and opportunity that exists within every situation.

We have to release the pain of judgment, guilt, and blame in order to see the silver lining that graces every cloud.

FREQUENCIES

Our human vibrations are sent out as frequencies, and those vibrations, or waves, are interpreted through our heart as emotions. Depending on your vibrational level and how you're physically and emotional tuned, you'll interpret the vibrations differently than someone else. The human ear receives frequencies and then converts them to sounds, thoughts, or feelings. These will trigger emotions based on your emotional filters. Our body receives the frequency, and the mind creates the emotion. At that point, we create ourselves with each emotion and thought. We are surrounded by an infinite number of frequencies. It's up to us to decide what we create from the experience.

KARMA

Some wonder if karma can be reversed. The simple answer is in a new question. Can the ripples in a pond be called back before they reach the other side? They cannot... you can create new ripples to merge with the past, but the actions of your past continually collide and co-create your future. The intensity of the ripples is a factor in the creation.

Doing what you do in life is just a means of experiencing who you really are. It's not so important what you do in life; it's what you learn about yourself through the experience that's the real point of our experiences. If we're not looking at our life with some higher purpose, then we'll continue to drift. I don't mean we drift physically; I mean that our identity will remain uncertain.

When you have a stable self-identity, it doesn't matter what you do in life. You're not defined by what you do. Your self-awareness will make every day a precious gift.

The shadows of uncertainty are illuminated
When the soul seeks the truth.

FAILURE?

The feeling of failure is a very simple state of mind and is an illusion. Our choices are karmic, and play out in a way that allows us to experience life through our thoughts, actions, and emotions. This platform allows for an infinite number of choices and potential outcomes for your life.

A more enlightened entity understands that any of the options would serve a great purpose in your personal evolution. You're at this place in your life right now, because there are experiences that need to be acquired to understand the next round of experiences.

That's why you're destined to repeat your "mistakes" if you don't learn from them. You can't create what you don't understand. If you don't, or can't appreciate the value of all of your experiences, then you're not consciously creating your life. You're just reacting to the situations around you.

The intense expression of gratitude for our life as it is, is the energy that calibrates your internal compass. This is where your gut feelings come into play. This is where inner peace comes from. It's the acknowledgment that all is as it should be.

Here's a good analogy for the value of each experience being in the order that they come: Look at math as an example. We wouldn't be able to understand algebra if we didn't first understand how to add, subtract, multiply and divide. We need a strong foundation of basic understanding to process any higher understanding. We must *learn* how to *learn* from our experiences. "Mistakes" are our tools for development.

> Y*our conviction is the force that sets the path*
> *And it is your will is that moves you through.*

O*ur world is set up perfectly, and it is only our perception that makes it seem difficult at times. Our individual view of the world is what shapes what we see. We can only see what we can imagine. We can only create what we can conceive.*

YOUR EVOLVING SPIRIT

Each time you leave a life experience from a conscious perspective (meaning that you understood the purpose of this experience), your next incarnation begins at a higher level. Your initial incarnations are often a bit of a struggle: they're very *physical* experiences. Gradually, each successive conscious incarnation will move you into a less physical and more conscious state of awareness. The purpose in this process is the evolution of your soul through the experiences of your lives.

We do this by acknowledging the value within each experience. The better we understand where we are in the process, the sooner we will understand the purpose of each experience and how we got there. It's necessary to move incrementally through each incarnation because there are vital life lessons that are embedded in each experience.

You wouldn't be capable of understanding a level without the acquired information from the previous experience anyway. Although each experience contains every possibility necessary to create your experience, there must be an understanding of how all the pieces come together in order to consciously create from it. Each incarnation in consciousness gives you a greater understanding of how you create.

OUR CHOICES

The confusing thing about "reality" is that the choices we've seemingly made can often seem very finite and forced; they may seem like choices we had to make, vs. something we'd like to do. Why does this seem normal? If someone were asking me that question, my reply would be something like this...

We make choices based on our level of consciousness. This means that our choices will be influenced by the outcome of our prior choices. If our choices have been rooted in fear and lack, then it's not likely that we'll create any new opportunities based in a higher plane of understanding. Understanding is all about awareness. We can't be aware of what we don't understand. The only way to understand is to desperately *want* to understand. You can't just wonder why things happen and never look any further. We can't keep making chaotic decisions and expect not to have chaos.

It's been said that once the pain of the present moment outweighs the pain of the unknown, then change will occur. People don't know what they don't know. Real change is seldom an option, because of the fear of the unknown, is worse than the present moment. This is a subconsciously driven reality. That's why when someone is finally sick enough of being sick, they'll make a change. They'll consider it a radical change because it's something they've never done before. The funny thing is, this *radical* change is nothing but a better choice. Life is simple in that way. When we stop building roadblocks, we can travel a lot smoother.

Here's a completely different way to look at all this. Not from a position of human suffering, but out of human potential. Imagine this scenario and deeply consider the implications. The following is much closer to reality than you may imagine.

Consider that there is a much more self-aware, multi-dimensional and infinite version of yourself that set up this life incarnation as a way for you to experience who you really are. Imagine that as you better handle each situation, you create better and better opportunities for yourself. Imagine that at the end of your life; you had the opportunity to review your life, not out of judgment, but as another opportunity to grow through your experiences. Now, imagine that every situation in front of you was created as an opportunity to experience yourself through that experience. This is where you become the conscious observer of your life. You have to willfully participate in the creation of your life. *You* are the only person that you have to impress. Drop the guilt of not being good enough. This is not about who did the best. This is simply an opportunity to expand your true self through living your life as only you can create it. Discover yourself while adding to the collective experience. You've imagined lots of things about yourself that were not true. Try imagining a life that truly has a purpose, and that purpose is inside you. Try to impress yourself and see what happens.

Healing happens when you let your heart open. Compassion is the force that will bring things back into harmony. Harmony is the balance of nature that sustains life and heals.

In this era of growing technology, we can see the infinitely small with our microscopes, and at the same time, the infinitely far with our telescopes. It's easy for us to see what's going on. The next phase of our evolution is to understand better what we see.

THOR, REBORN IN CONSCIOUSNESS.

Let's use the analogy of the mythological character of Thor, as he's cast out of the kingdom. Once he realized his faults and transformed himself through compassionate acts of selflessness, he began to see life as an opportunity to share his uniqueness with others. He could now see the higher purpose in his life.

Now reborn in consciousness, he was able to rejoin his kingdom, a new man, reborn by his own conscious actions. Now fulfilled in spirit by the recognition of his purpose. He now *realizes* that limitations are perceptions that can be re-written through our conscious awareness. The quantum realization of our true self, capable of anything and accountable for everything, is how we are "saved" from the blindness of our ignorance.

THE PATTERNS AROUND US

Practice in developing one's awareness can be as simple as learning to recognize the patterns around us. It's easier to recognize patterns when we know they exist and we're consciously looking for them. As with most things in life, if we're not paying attention, we're not likely to experience anything of real value. This is the auto pilot mode most people are stuck in. They're just moving about their day, while not absorbing much of anything consciously. Awareness of one's surroundings is a good place to start looking and listening, for things that may be providing direction. Like building any puzzle, we have to look for pieces that go together.

This is a very conscious effort. When we use this same approach to living, we can begin to sort through what we don't need or want and begin to look for things that we *do* want. As we acquire more and more pieces to work with, we can see that there are an infinite number of options to take. The "Big Picture" becomes much clearer when we start pulling these pieces together. The first step is knowing that we can, and should, look for more options. The next step is "seeing" what's around you, and pulling it all together. You'll be amazed what you'll see when you start looking. The beauty around us is staggering. If you'll focus your attention on just about anything and let yourself experience it, not judge it, you'll experience the perfection within it. This feeling will be the beginning of new awareness. Applying this new state awareness to all dimensions of your life will certainly broaden your sense of self, and, open a channel to your higher self.

Once you're steady on your path, your angels will rush to guide you further. Your initial enthusiasm is what triggers movement.
Your physical movement, as well as your thought energy provide the waves of energy that carry your dreams towards reality.

Our personal gifts to be opened may be finite, but there are implications and influence will go on forever. That's why our gifts must be opened. Our gifts only magnify who we are, so if we live a life that's unrealized, understand that that was only from our fear of discovery. Our gifts are to be shared... that's how we all grow.

Just like our eyes can only see visible light, our awareness is a fairly narrow spectrum of information. Our general *State of Being* is drawn from this narrow perspective; this perspective is what forms the basis for our judgments. This is why it's important to first broaden your state of mind and seek the deeper nature of things. It's the accumulation of conscious experiences that elevate our perspective, and then our new State of Being is in higher Awareness.

Once you see the patterns in life, your choices become clearer.

When you live life seeking the truth, you find yourself.

Quieting the mind allows you to experience the truth.

Your actions are a reflection of your state of consciousness.
The world that you create around you will be a reflection
of your true self.

In a successful relationship, you should feel connected, but not
tethered. The ability to move around gives you the freedom to
grow. If you feel tethered, you will feel trapped or held back.
Deep down you already know if you're in the right place or
not. Denial holds you back. Fear keeps you there.

Opposites seem to attract out of need...

You don't have to be proud of everything you've done,
just be proud of the direction you're going.
That's how you gauge your course.

Don't settle for a story... look for the truth.

When we move with awareness, we create with purpose. When we stop making bold moves, we stop moving much at all.

HEALING

There is no healing without accountability. You don't have to expose yourself to the world, but you must be honest with yourself. Once you do, then healing will begin. You may have relationships to mend, but that will come out of the joy of awakening, not out of obligation. Your life can now seek its purpose. It's no longer about how you lived your life; it's about how you're living it. When we stop beating ourselves up and start building ourselves up, we can begin the healing process.

TOXIC ENERGY

There is undeniably enough toxic energy in certain types of *heavy* music, videos and games, to substantially affect the universal mind. There is a great deal of pain broadcast into the universe, and that energy will ultimately manifest itself somewhere. That somewhere can only be in *one's* life. The attraction to that type of music is derived from the resonance of mutual energy. If you're attracted to it, it's because you feel it, it moves you. We don't have the same frequency all the time, but you can gauge your energy by the majority of the things that do move you. You are responsible for what you allow in your life.

Conviction is what brings thought to its full potential.

Change does not constitute growth
until the change is made, Consciously.

Belief requires memory. Creation requires action.

SCIENCE VERSUS SPIRITUALITY

Here's the thing about Science versus Spirituality, "Experimental vs. Experiential." Physicist, Stephen Hawking concluded, that even by acknowledging the interconnectedness of all space/time and energy, that there is nothing that exists within any "Divine" realm beyond that.

As brilliant and admired as Mr. Hawking's is, that he has, in my opinion, had no significant experiential relationship that would compel him to emotionally grasp the Divine realm and experience. The divine realm is entirely experiential. Given that, without a diverse and objective perspective of understanding, even our "divine experiences" can be quickly dismissed, or mentally accredited to personal religious teachings/beliefs. Meaning, that depending on your Religion, your mind justifies the experience to fit that paradigm, it's like a placebo effect. The placebo effect is the result of belief, and our minds manifest what we believe to be real. When your mind, your body, and your vibrational focus are in harmony, regardless of your religion, miracles will happen.

My belief is that Mr. Hawking's contribution and purpose for this life experience was to bring forth, expand, and scientifically confirm the interconnected nature of energy and scientifically quantify the general nature of what we consider life. In this, I believe he has succeeded. There is no need, in my mind, for either Science or Spirituality, to prove one another. In my mind, they are simply two sides of the same coin. They are two ways to conceive one reality. The paradox is that being firmly on one side, obscures the ability to see the other side. You have to want to see what's on the other side and then make an effort to see it.

At this point, it doesn't matter what your current perspective is. You're right where you need to be, for now. Someday you'll, "need more information" or "feel something inside," that compels you to look around the forbidden corner for more answers. For now, just know that there will always be more to discover about yourself and what you're a part of.

Your peace of mind lies within you. Happiness is a choice.
In your quest for more… look inside first.

In divining the truth, look for the most peaceful source.
The bully is not likely to tell the truth.

When Shakespeare says, "All the world is a stage,"
Please take it to heart, that we're here to engage.
To transcend the pain, and to be humble in glory…
and the point of this life? It's the journey, and not the story.

It often takes more strength to let go, than to cling tightly.

Are you a living example of your beliefs or are you a living example of your creations? The difference is in consciousness.

Contemplation provides the mental and emotional space required for change. It's the conscious act of contemplation that gives you the opportunity to reconcile the contrasts within your life.

Our View of the World

The paradigm that most people live within," their comfort zone," is often a fairly narrow view of the world; it's fairly safe and predictable. When one experiences something outside their comfort zone, it stirs something inside them. This stir is some level of fear. Our mind has difficulty processing things that are significantly outside of our paradigm. For example, the experiences that people might call hallucinations are most likely visions that the psyche can't understand. Some people would describe this sort of experience as "a bad trip," if it were part of a chemical experimentation.

Most of these substances don't create hallucinations, but rather, they expand our world of limited boundaries to the point of confusion. When the mind exceeds its sense of reality, it experiences fear. This is when we retreat into our comfort zone. It requires a great deal of soul searching to push past the fear of uncertainty. This is why the evolution of the soul requires many lifetimes.

The process of understanding the underlying nature of life is indeed a process and must be experienced. The explanations from one person to another are only a glimpse of the reality. One's personal experience, preceded by a desire to see more clearly, is the only path to enlightenment. Each new step towards understanding one's self expands not only your experiences, but it expands the world around you.

There have been many great explorers of science and the human mind. Einstein, Da Vinci, Galileo, are just a few of many great minds that acknowledged their inspiration did not come from rational thought; it came from beyond their rational minds.

Spiritual teachers throughout history have told us that we are more than our bodies. We are infinitely joined throughout eternity through consciousness. We are creators of this life through our will to exist. Our opportunity, in this life, is to discover our true selves and explore the infinite potential inherent in each one of us. Just know that there is far more to life that you can ever imagine. All you have to do is be bold enough to experience what it is.

Yin and yang create the field of dimension that we live within; it's this contrast that adds depth to our experience.

To deny ones' inherent nature is to miss the opportunity to experience ones' true self.

There are three elements in your life that have to work together to move in the direction you want. Your intention, your purpose, and the other... integrity. These things working together create the congruency that makes them work synchronically. Like gears in a watch, everything must move together to move at all. Otherwise, they are frozen in time.

Living consciously requires a re-calibration of your senses. Your old beliefs, fears, and perceptions have clouded and dulled your ability to feel the truth. As we release our attachments to the past, we can look forward with new awareness, clarity, and inner peace.

INTELLIGENCE

It seems that while assessing intelligence one must consider what the standards are. I would say that intellectual intelligence is surface level. This means that this person is adept at evaluating a perceived problem, based on linear facts. The next level of intelligence is psychological intelligence. This person would be able to see the subconscious driving force behind the surface actions. The next level of intelligence relates to spiritual psychology. This person pays very little attention to the surface level conditions, and even sees past the underlying subconscious issues, and clearly sees the higher purpose of the experience, not only for our physical self but for our souls' purpose. There are many levels that we exist on simultaneously, and when we live consciously, we feed them all.

For over twenty years I've gathered information in the form of new perspectives. The pictures that they form are multidimensional and holographic in nature. There are no combinations of any of this information that creates any one-dimensional point of view. The world that we live in is a spectacular wave of potential. Each piece of new information is intertwined and supported in all directions. The universe that we see with our eyes is only one dimension of this evolving experience. The universe that we don't see is another. When we combine the seen with the unseen, we create infinite dimensions of possible realities. Each of these realities is a piece of the big picture. The intention is not to complete the puzzle; it's to create it.

When our imagination exceeds our sense of reality,

we experience fear.

THE GREAT TEACHERS

The Buddha said, "He, who sees me, sees the teaching, and he who sees the teaching, sees me." Jesus said, "He that believeth in me, shall have everlasting life."

Given that both statements are translations and interpretations, I believe that the essence and purpose of these teachings are the same. It's to the degree that we feel separateness, that we experience pain.

Jesus and the Buddha were both great teachers, and both were trying to share their understanding of enlightenment, and that separateness of spirit is an illusion.

Jesus stated, "He who believeth in me, the works that I do, he will also do, and greater works than these he will also do." The interpretation that best correlates with much earlier teachings is that we are each capable of miracles and creating our own destiny, through higher spiritual awareness; thus discovering our own divinity.

Enlightenment is an internal process of awakening, not a gift to behold. When Jesus says, "Seek ye first the kingdom of God, and his righteousness, and all these things shall be added unto you," he is instructing you to seek the truth, to seek a higher level of enlightenment and purpose. The Buddha teaches that there is no knowledge without sacrifice. Meaning that without having walked the journey, the path is just a fabled story.

The great Masters teach that it's through our diligent effort, that the kingdom is revealed, not by belief. The Buddha and Jesus were both teachers of the way to enlightenment, not the givers of fruit, without planting a seed.

The Buddha says, "One must lose everything in order to receive anything." He is referring to our ego-centered attachments and beliefs. I've heard it stated in another way as well, "it's hard to fill a cup that's already full." As long as we think that we already have the answers, there is no room for anything else. Until you seek the truth and are open to receive, your *belief* is but a life jacket that promises to keep you afloat.

Be eternally grateful for what you don't understand right now, and then seek to experience it.

Each moment in darkness is an opportunity in faith.
(In yourself)

The beauty of being awake is choosing your reality…
instead of Accepting one.

A conflict is resolved once its purpose is understood.

Religions offer a finite reality of life. Life does not need religion for its existence, but religion needs to preach the promise of eternal life, for it to exist.

THE UNIVERSE

The universe doesn't care what you believe; it just responds to what you do believe. Much like the quote from Henry Ford: "Whether you believe you can, or believe you can't, you're correct either way."

Divine harmony is the essence of the spiritual engine. When your mind, your body, and your vibrational focus is in harmony with the universal mind, (God), we move with the flow of universal energy. This is when, what we experience as miracles, happens.

Your mind is sort of like a piece of a hologram. It has its personal identity and individual significance but also has an awareness of its connection to everything. Each thought is a pathway to another thought and to any point in time. This is how we communicate through dimensions. We manifest ourselves as we focus our attention. Each piece embodies the sum of the whole, simply by shifting the focus of consciousness.

This is what Jesus, Buddha, and many other fully realized Masters have been trying to teach for thousands of years. In the East, the original intent of these teachings is closer to the truth than what has been taught in the west. The West has grossly twisted the original messages, and there's very little of original intent left behind in them.

Here's a good gauge for divining the truth. If there is any

level of fear built into a profits message, it can't be part of a divinely derived message. Life exists because it's compelled to exist, not because it's commanded to. There's no logic in fear. Life creates, and sustains itself, through a process of co-creation. The processes and the purposes of life are to recreate itself through an ever-evolving cycle of experiences. This process of re-creation is a totally harmonious one. These processes have a beginning and an end… a life and a death.

Life does not need to be afraid of something to exist or re-create itself. Life wouldn't serve any real purpose if our existence were based on achieving or conforming to a single belief. If you have chosen to conform, your decisions were rooted in fear. It couldn't be any other way. Fear and creation aren't just opposites; there's an even bigger difference between them. Fear is an illusion, and creation is all that there is.

WHAT WE DON'T KNOW

Most of us are operating under a finite illusion that is keeping us from even imagining that there's something else to consider. To grow, we have first to acknowledge that what we don't know is infinite. We should embrace this infinite unknowing, as the beginning of our new awareness. We must first replace the comfort of our excepted knowledge, with the passion for discovering what we don't yet understand.

Our comfort should reside in the radiant glow of the great unknown, the quest itself. Not the quest for happiness, but the quest to see, and embrace the perfection of the experience that we exist within right now. There is an inherent perfection within every experience. Part of our life's purpose is to simply embody these experiences without judgment, and grow *with* the experience without resistance.

Resistance literally applies the breaks to your life. When you release the resistance, you can start to move; this is what creates flow. When your life begins to flow, you'll begin to see your true self, emerge. The synchronicities of life will become your guideposts. Your path will open, and your purpose will unfold. This is how we grow. It's time to release your fears and experience who you really are. You are the actual gift of creation itself

WE CAN MAKE A DIFFERENCE

Nowadays, it seems that our political agendas and lifestyles have become the new benchmark for whether or not we go to war. The "defense of our lifestyle" has been disguised as the "Defense of our Nation." Our need for more and more resources should be telling us that we need to make some changes, or at the very least, make better choices. We've let our visceral desires take control of our moral compasses.

Balance is, and forever will be, the benchmark for sustainability. Without balance, there will always be a *tilt* that will eventually slide, downhill. We may not have grown up with the greatest examples, but there is an innate level of humanity and compassion within each one of us. We may have lost our way, but we haven't lost who we really are. Our nature to live is second only to our nature to love. When we finally awaken to the consequences of our unconscious actions, we can then follow our true nature back to a path of compassion and sustainability.

This book is about seeing things differently, much like when Galileo first looked at the heavens through a telescope, or when scientists first realized that microscopes could see into tiny unknown worlds. These simple shifts in perspectives forever changed what we know about ourselves. What we accept as truth today, would have been blasphemy and cost us our lives only a few hundred years ago. It has taken hundreds, if not thousands of years, for some people to let go of the past and their long-held beliefs of *tradition*. Before we can see something in its true nature, we often project it as an idea or belief. These beliefs become battles fought with our bodies and minds. Seeing the truth requires a shift in perception, a new lens, and a willingness to see past your long-held beliefs. It may also require a reassessment of what you hold dear.

To seek the truth, you must look deeply at the world around you and question why things are the way they are. In the movie, "A Few Good Men," there's a quote from the commander that's being deposed, "You can't handle the truth," he says. For many, this is the honest truth. If your comfort lies in faith, then you're likely paralyzed by the past. Truth is about discovery, and with discovery comes change. When we experience these new realities, our world begins to broaden, and we evolve through our discoveries. This can only happen when we *want* to see the truth. The quest of self-discovery is about seeking your purpose and your higher self. To understand the answers, you'll have to accept a new paradigm of reality. "When The Student Is Ready" is a perspective through a different lens; a lens focused on discovery, not on an agenda. As you open your heart, you'll be guided in many directions that all lead to the truth. Part of this new paradigm is finding out that there is no failure in life; it's not about pass or fail. All experiences and all paths serve a higher purpose. As you discover your true self, you'll begin to see the big picture. We are all one in this experience, and we all matter.

There are two things that we all must do in this lifetime to move forward. One of them is to be a good student, and the other is to be a good teacher. Both should be full-time jobs. Not out of obligation, but out of a swelling, internal commitment to the discovery of our true self. With this commitment, comes an immense compassion for life and a glowing inner awareness. This give and take, this yin and yang, is what creates the balance that supports our purpose for this life experience. Living in this way is walking the walk. When one realizes the nature and function of each life experience, as the student *and* as the teacher, the illusion of separateness fades away. When we experience our life equally as the student, and as the teacher, we create balance. The teacher in us provides clarity and compassion, as the student in ourselves awakens through an evolving gratitude for all life. This nurturing balance is the creative force itself. As we open our hearts, love and compassion will soon replace the fear that has held us back. As we begin to feel again, we begin to live again.

Thank you so much for sharing this experience with me. I'm very grateful for the opportunity to share this time with you, and I wish you all the very best on your journey through self-discovery.

Remember to be grateful for each and every moment and know you're right where you need to be... for now ☺

To My Daughters

This place that we share, one world if you dare,
Seems like two places, me here and you there.

We can share in this world, with a shift of our vision,
then see for ourselves, there is no division.

We exist as souls, with a mind and a source,
but we often get lost, from our purpose and course.

When we see these divisions as false, with illusion,
we can experience our life, with this new conclusion:

As we see only love, in this life we embrace,
We'll feel in ourselves, this connection in space.

This gift that we share, this connection in time,
Offers these moments, so precious, divine.

See we are never apart, in my heart this is true,
Forever and always, my love is with you.

Dad

Thank you so much for sharing this journey.

The quest for enlightenment is as old as consciousness itself. Our desire to fulfill our true nature will always drive us towards our chosen purpose.

If you feel moved to help share in this journey, writing a review through Amazon will help others on their quest towards personal enrichment. When we all work together, we all grow together.

To write a review go to: Amazon.com
Search for Michael E Clarke
Click on When the Student is Ready and
scroll down to reviews. Choose write a review.

Thanks again for taking the time
to share in this journey ☺

www.ingramcontent.com/pod-product-compliance
Lightning Source LLC
LaVergne TN
LVHW091217080426
835509LV00009B/1046